10 BRANCHES OF GROWTH

REAL-LIFE PRODUCTIVITY FOR A FRUITFUL LIFE

KALEN BRUCE

CONTENTS

Acknowledgments   v
Introduction   ix

1. Character   1
2. Discipline   15
3. Action   33
4. Habits   37
5. Energy   53
6. Time   61
7. Wealth   87
8. Seasons   107
9. Self   121
10. God   135

Afterword   167
Recommended Reading   169
About the Author   171
Notes   173

Copyright © 2020 by Kalen Bruce.

All rights reserved. No part of this work may be reproduced, distributed, or transmitted in any form or by any means, without prior written permission.

For permission to use any part of this work, please contact the author at freedomsprout.com.

ISBN: 978-1-7349734-0-2

Library of Congress Control Number: 2020907633

All content reflects the author's opinion at a given time and can change as time progresses. All information should be taken as an opinion and should not be misconstrued for professional or legal advice. The contents of this book are informational in nature and are not legal or tax advice, and the author is not engaged in the provision of legal, tax, or any other advice.

The views presented in this book are those of the author and do not necessarily represent the views of DoD or its components.

Scripture quotations are from the ESV® Bible (The Holy Bible, English Standard Version®), copyright © 2001 by Crossway Bibles, a publishing ministry of Good News Publishers. Used by permission. All rights reserved.

Cover photo by Darwin Vegher.

Printed by Kalen Bruce in the United States of America.

First printing edition 2020. Hot Springs, Arkansas.

ACKNOWLEDGMENTS

A special thanks to everyone who influenced me over the years. I am the man I am today because of God, and the Godly men and women who helped mold me along the way. Also, thank you to my wife, Tiffany, for putting up with my ridiculous predawn hours, and allowing me the time to write books such as this one. You drive me to be a better version of myself every day.

To my five children: Abi, Asher, Hannah, Jezreel, and Josiah. Without you guys, I would have no reason to write these things down.

INTRODUCTION

This is a short manual on living a life of growth.

You have to make your own choices. You have to find what works for you. This book is packed full of practical and actionable ideas. I don't want to be vague; I want to give you strategies you can actually implement.

This book is brief, but even if it were the size of the Encyclopedia Britannica, it couldn't possibly tell you everything you need to know about life. Many of your lessons will come from life itself. You have to decide who you want to be, what you want to do with your life, and the outcome you're looking for. My hope is that this book will influence you in a positive way, but you're the only one who can actually live your life. You *determine* how you live your life. Don't let anyone tell you differently.

The choice is yours.

This book is a whole-life productivity system. Productivity doesn't end with lifehacks, the latest apps, and new ways to organize. True productivity bleeds into every area of your life. It's a mindset. A lifestyle. That's why you need a total productivity system you can live out each day.

I'm going to dive into 10 areas of your life. 10 different branches of your life that you will continue to grow in for the rest of your life. If you master how you handle these 10 areas (not that any of us will ever *fully* master them), you will be in control of your own life. Never stop growing.

One final note: This book is short because it's direct. Direct can easily translate to offensive for some people. If you're easily offended, and don't like to seriously think about where you're at with some areas of life, you may want to stop at this page. If you understand that we, as human beings, aren't perfect, but we can grow and become significantly better, then keep reading. Just be ready to do some self-reflection. We all need to be doing that regularly.

Summary, Action, Reflection

Each chapter will end with a summary, which includes three questions to ask yourself about what you just read. Asking questions can be the best way to apply new information in our lives.

After the three questions, there will be an action step. This is a short paragraph with something you can immediately implement, based on the chapter you just read. Take these seriously.

Finally, there is a spot for reflection. This is for you to write down any notes, and capture thoughts, about things that resonated with you in the chapter. Use this space as soon as you finish reading, so the information is still fresh in your mind. I know most people won't write in the actual book, in the small space at the end of each chapter. So think of this area as more of a prompt to take notes in whichever way you wish.

Now let's dive into a real-life productivity system for a fruitful life...

1
CHARACTER

Character is the sum of qualities that defines a person. What defines you? Your discipline, habits, and how you spend your time. That's what defines you, whether you like it or not.

Show me where your time goes, and I'll show you where your heart is. Is it where you want it to be? Do your actions line up with your beliefs? Do you do the right thing, whether people are looking or not? Or do you do things differently, depending on who you're doing them for, or in front of?

The concept of character is woven throughout this entire book. Still, it's important to talk about it first, because it will determine how you handle the rest of this book. Let's look at the chapters coming up:

- **Discipline** – Your level of self-discipline is directly related to your character. Do you do the hard things? Do you practice self-discipline on a daily basis?

- **Action** – Not only the way you act, but the action you put into every day, defines your character.
- **Habits** – The entirety of your habits make up who you are. Your habits are the things you do, day in, and day out.
- **Energy** – Your energy level isn't always going to match the level of action you wish to take. Your character will determine the choice you make it those un-energetic times.
- **Time** – You spend your time doing what matters to you. Does that line up with your overall idea of character?
- **Wealth** – Do you want wealth for the right reasons?
- **Seasons** – Life is full of seasons. You'll go through plenty. You've been through plenty. How you respond to those seasons will be determined by your character.
- **Self** – You are your character. It defines you to others.
- **God** – If your character and values aren't derived from something higher than yourself, you're going to fail people… often.

Character is about honesty. It's about living in private as you speak in public. It's about self-sacrifice. It's about making truth the foundation of your life. It's about avoiding distractions from the unimportant things and focusing on the important. It's about forgiving others when they've wronged you. It's about knowing and doing the right thing.

You know the basics of character, so let's talk about a couple of the qualities we can quantify: grit and excuses. These are two areas you can easily fail in if your character is weak, yet they're two areas you can master to succeed at anything.

Grit

The word "grit" is getting a new identity. It's not just about cowboys anymore. It's being used in the psychological sense more and more — mental grit.

Grit is defined as, "firmness of mind or spirit : unyielding courage in the face of hardship or danger." In Psychology, Grit is defined as, "a positive, non-cognitive trait based on an individual's perseverance of effort combined with the passion for a particular long-term goal or end state (a powerful motivation to achieve an objective)."

Angela Duckworth's research on grit leads the way, so let's turn to the experts. She's the author of a book titled, *Grit: The Power of Passion and Perseverance*, and she's been studying the idea for years. Cindra Kamphoff wrote somewhat of a sequel to that book; it's called, *Beyond Grit: Ten Powerful Practices to Gain the High-Performance Edge*. I recommend reading both.

Other than compassion and a charitable heart, grit may be the most essential character trait you can learn, *and it can be learned*. The successful people of the world rarely did it on intelligence alone, and many of the *most* successful people admit they aren't the smartest, but they're the grittiest in one way or another. So how are grit and perseverance *learned*? You can start with a few practices. It's a process.

Reframe Failure

Mistakes and failures are some of the most excellent teachers, if we frame them that way. You don't have to use cheesy (but often helpful) phrases like "fail forward" to make this effective. It's the simple act of embracing failure as a positive thing and learning from it.

Welcome Challenge

Successful people who came from broken childhoods often feel sorry for kids who are raised in a good home, because they never got the opportunity to deal with adversity. That's why some of the most successful and happiest people had the worst childhoods. Even if you weren't raised in an adverse environment, you have to allow challenge into your life. Don't always take the easy path.

Take Encouragement

Encouragement has to come along with learning from failure and handling challenges. Find people who encourage you along the way, but who also teach you hard lessons, and don't let you off the hook when you mess up. Sure, failure and challenges will tear you down a little, but you must find people who encourage you to try 10x harder next time.

If you follow the pattern, you will see failure in a positive light. You'll accept the challenge, fail, learn from the failure, overcome obstacles, and fully accept encouragement along the way.

Grit seems to be the common denominator between successful people. The ability to focus on, and achieve a goal, is not common. Grit is what separates those who do from those who merely talk. Building grit, or mental toughness, takes time. It's hard. There's no shortcut. And most importantly, let there be no excuses.

Excuses

Excuses are funny, because we notice them more from others than from ourselves. Why's it important to talk about excuses? Because excuses may be hindering you more than you could ever know. We all have an excuse for something, somewhere in our life. Track down where you're relying on excuses, and see how to change that area of your life.

> *"But they all alike began to make excuses. The first said to him, 'I have bought a field, and I must go out and see it. Please have me excused.' And another said, 'I have bought five yoke of oxen, and I go to examine them. Please have me excused.' And another said, 'I have married a wife, and therefore I cannot come.'"*
>
> — LUKE 14:18-20

What truly separates the unsuccessful from the successful? Excuses. Successful people fail as much or more than unsuccessful people, because they are determined. They know how to get back up and try again, perhaps in a different way, but...again. Failure doesn't slow them down, it motivates them. Unsuccessful people like to make excuses and explain *why* they can't do it. Successful people either do it, or they try again until they do it.

We all have an excuse. If we really want to devote our mind and energy to it, we will always be able to think of a reason we can't do something. Moses watched God do amazing things—that were only possible with God—yet he still made excuses when God asked him to speak to Pharaoh:

> *"But Moses said to the Lord, "Oh, my Lord, I am not eloquent, either in the past or since you have spoken to your servant, but I am slow of speech and of tongue." Then the Lord said to him, "Who has made man's mouth? Who makes him mute, or deaf, or seeing, or blind? Is it not I, the Lord? Now therefore go, and I will be with your mouth and teach you what you shall speak." But he said, "Oh, my Lord, please send someone else." Then the anger of the Lord was kindled against Moses and he said, "Is there not Aaron, your brother, the Levite? I know that he can speak well. Behold, he is coming out to meet you, and when he sees you, he will be glad in his heart."*

— Exodus 4:10-14

Excuses have been around since before Moses. In fact, the first thing Adam did after eating the forbidden fruit was give an excuse as to why it was Eve's fault, and Eve explained why it was the serpent's fault (Genesis 3). Excuses are often disguised as negative thinking, or "reasons," instead of what they actually are... useless excuses. We always like to think our situation is different. It's not.

Overcome the excuses you devise and follow through with your true aspirations in life. If we all let excuses stop us from achieving what we were meant for, God's work would be left undone. It doesn't matter how legitimate the excuse is, excuses help nothing and hold us back from everything.

We aren't responsible for what happens to us, but we are responsible for how we respond to it. We like to think of our excuses as "valid reasons," but the fact is, we are still forming excuses, and we get no benefit from them, even if we can validate them. If you feel like you have valid reasons instead of excuses, consider this...

Life Without Limbs

Nick Vujicic is a Christian evangelist and speaker, born with tetra-amelia syndrome, a rare disorder characterized by the absence of all four limbs, hence the name of his company: Life Without Limbs, Inc.. Do you think Nick has a few good, legitimate excuses for why he can't do some things? Sure, he could come up with more excuses than you or I could, based on the situation he was dealt. But does he? Absolutely not. That's his entire purpose behind his motivational speaking and teaching.

We all have a tendency to compare our weaknesses to other people's strengths. What good is that? How does that improve our situation? Here's what Nick says about comparing ourselves to others, especially our sufferings (which is where excuses usually come from):

> "We can't, and we should not, compare sufferings. We come together as a family of God, hand in hand. And then together coming and standing upon the promises of God, knowing that no matter who you are, no matter what you're going through, that God knows it, He is with you, He is going to pull you through."

God can and will pull us through anything, but it's easy to forget that when we're in the moment of adversity. We also tend to dwell on the past. Excuses come from past experiences; they don't come from the future. That's why Nick says, "Don't put your life on hold so that you can dwell on the unfairness of past hurts."

If a man with tetra-amelia syndrome doesn't dwell on the past and what life has given him, why should we? Excuses will only hold you back from anything and everything. There really is no such thing as a good excuse. Let's forget about excuses, no matter how bad it may seem, and focus on what we can change and what we can do. As Nick puts it...

> "Have you ever felt trapped in circumstances, then discovered that the only trap was your own lack of vision, lack of courage, or failure to see that you had better options?"

It's easy to see why we *can't* do things. We like to give other people the benefit of the doubt, while we sit back and think, "I could never do that." But the truth is, the one who did it has thought, at some point, that they couldn't. Anyone who has accomplished something amazing went through a point where they felt like they weren't going to be able to do it. It's human nature.

No Test, No Testimony

"No test, no testimony" may sound like a cliché bumper sticker, but it's true: the most inspiring testimonies have been a result of the most challenging tests. People have built huge businesses and served God in outstanding ways with disabilities, financial struggles, or other obstacles.

Can you do the same? Absolutely. But you've got to stop making excuses and take responsibility for your life. We can all do huge things if we accept where we're at and press on toward the goal. Look at what Paul says in his letter to the Philippians. He addresses the issue of not being perfect and not being in the best situation, but the best time to start pressing forward is today. This goes for your relationship with Jesus and achieving the goals you want to achieve. Here's how Paul put it:

> *"Not that I have already obtained this or am already perfect, but I press on to make it my own, because Christ Jesus has made me his own. Brothers, I do not consider that I have made it my own. But one thing I do: forgetting what lies behind and straining forward to what lies ahead, I press on toward the goal for the prize of the upward call of God in Christ Jesus. Let those of us who are mature think this way, and if in anything you think otherwise, God will reveal that also to you. Only let us hold true to what we have attained."*
>
> — PHILIPPIANS 3:12-16

Did you get that message? We are to keep pressing toward the goal. Don't let your situation define you, and don't let excuses get in your way. When we continue to use an excuse, we validate it more and more. Let's stop validating our excuses, and start taking action on our goals.

Whatever you want to do in life, you can do it, but that's the thing... you have to actually do it. Nothing will hold you back unless you let it. What do you ultimately want? What's your end goal? An international ministry? A successful business or organization that helps millions of people? Enough money to fund mission trips all over the world or feed millions of hungry people?

What is it? And can you do it? Of course...

- **Can you do it if you have a physical handicap?** Nick Vujicic proved you can.

- **Can you do it if you have a speech disorder?** Moses proved you can.
- **Can you do it if you have a reading disorder?** Albert Einstein, Richard Branson, Jim Carrey, and countless others who had dyslexia proved you can.
- **Can you do it if you're a single parent?** Angela Benton, founder and CEO of NewME, has accelerated over 300 startups and helped them raise over $17 million in funding, despite being a single mom since she was 16.
- **Can you do it if you have a full house?** Ask the Duggars. My wife and I have five children and haven't sacrificed a thing (including time with them). You can also look to many successful politicians, as they seem to love big families, and kissing babies.
- **Can you do it if you have failed before?** Thomas Edison failed at creating the light bulb more than 1,000 times before he succeeded. Stephen King's first novel was rejected 30 times before he went on to sell millions of books. Peter denied Jesus three times before going on to do amazing work as an apostle; he even wrote part of the New Testament.
- **Can you do it without God?** Sure, plenty of people have proved it's possible to have worldly success without God, but why would you? Many people feel like they've achieved success without God, but that really depends on their definition of success. Life is so much

more difficult without God. It's not easy being a Christian. In fact, it's one of the most difficult things I've done and continue to do daily. Most things that are worth anything are not easy, and a personal relationship with Jesus Christ is worth everything.

You don't need God to have money or business success; however, if you truly want to be successful, you're only going to find that in Christ...

"For those who live according to the flesh set their minds on the things of the flesh, but those who live according to the Spirit set their minds on the things of the Spirit. For to set the mind on the flesh is death, but to set the mind on the Spirit is life and peace. For the mind that is set on the flesh is hostile to God, for it does not submit to God's law; indeed, it cannot."

— Romans 8:5-7

What does success mean to you? Are your goals in line with your view of success? Once they are, ask yourself this question:

"What's stopping me from succeeding?"

Then do a character check. Do you act in accordance with how you believe?

Devote everything to your vision of success. Success may mean a strong relationship with Jesus and a happy family. Success may mean a successful business. Success could also mean a gigantic ministry. Whatever it is, make sure your goals line up with your idea of success, and make sure your idea of success lines up with God's Word. If you think you're failing, you might just be too busy making excuses to see the success you do have, and the success you're capable of achieving.

So what now? Well, it's time to take action, of course. Reading about building character and being successful is great, but you must put a plan into action if you want to actually make it happen.

Summary & Action

Where you spend your time reveals your character.

- *Do you spend your time in accordance with your character?*

Grit separates the people who do from the people who talk.

- *Do you have grit? Do you allow challenge? Do you embrace failure?*

Excuses provide no value.

- *Do you make excuses? Do you feel like you have "good excuses?"*

Action: Go 30 days without making a single excuse. Let your yes be yes and your no be no (Matthew 5:37). It won't be easy. You may surprise yourself at how many excuses you make and how often.

Reflection:

2

DISCIPLINE

Motivation is nice, but it's also highly overrated. If you think you're going to be motivated to do everything you have to do, when you have to do it, you'll be disappointed. Motivation is fleeting.

There is a force working against you. In his book, *The War of Art*, Stephen Pressfield refers to this as, "The Resistance." Capitalized to show the true nature of this beast. Stephen puts it this way:

> "Rule of thumb: The more important a call or action is to our soul's evolution, the more Resistance we will feel toward pursuing it."

What is The Resistance? It's anything that gets in between you and what you're trying to accomplish. It could be tiredness, lack of motivation, distraction, or even a friend or family member.

Pressfield explains The Resistance as a real force at work in the universe. If you're doing what you feel like you're called to do, there will be something trying to stop you. You've felt it before. You plan to do something you know you *should* do, and something happens. Or your motivation completely leaves you. Or something more important just so happens to come up. Or... you know the feeling.

There will always be something trying to stop you from accomplishing what you've set out to accomplish. We all get sidetracked. Being aware of it, when it happens, is the first step to handling it. If you acknowledge each time you "don't feel like it" or each time something seems to "just come up," you can begin to handle The Resistance.

Bring Back Discipline

Discipline is one of the greatest forces in the universe. You may consider yourself disciplined, or far from it, but the point is, it's important. Generations before now seemed to preach the importance of discipline, but often there was no "why." How many people do you know who were taught the importance of discipline without being taught the value? You may be one of them.

All too often, we think of discipline as torture. "If it doesn't feel good, and it isn't fun, it must be building discipline." Maybe you haven't said this out loud, but that's the essence of how we view discipline. It doesn't have to be like that. There is a purpose for building discipline beyond merely being "tough."

Discipline is one of the keys to a fulfilled life. It may

seem like there is freedom in doing whatever you feel like doing, but it's actually the other way around. Setting restrictions and parameters in your life, and holding yourself accountable through self-discipline, is the start of truly being free – free to live the life you want. If you try to do it without discipline, you won't go far.

Think of discipline like a muscle. You have a discipline muscle that can be trained and strengthened. Regardless of how you view your level of discipline right now, you can increase it. A common question is, "Is discipline an ability some people are born with and some aren't, or can it be built in anyone's life?"

Well, let's talk about that...

Born or Built?

Once you've decided to commit to discipline, one of the first negative thoughts that may pop into your head is that discipline can't be created. You may be thinking it comes to some and passes over others, but that's not true at all.

Discipline can be created.

In fact, I would argue that people who seem to have "born discipline" actually derived discipline from their environment as a child. Is it nature or nurture? A little bit of both, but even the studies that link discipline genetically overlook the fact that a parent who knows the value of discipline is more likely to teach their child the value of discipline. This isn't hard for me to understand, because I grew up with almost no discipline at all, other than in one area.

As a kid, I enjoyed my summer vacations by playing

video games all day in the confines of my own room. However, I didn't always play inside; I loved to explore the great outdoors, and I did, whenever I wanted. When the school year showed back up, I couldn't devote my days to whatever I wanted anymore, except when I decided to play sick and stay home. I don't think there was a single time I pretended to be sick, and didn't get to stay home, and this carried over into high school. The difference in high school was that I stopped playing sick and just decided to only come to school when I felt like it. Believe it or not, I usually didn't feel like it at all.

When I was found out, I was able to find excuses and cover for myself, which got me out of any repercussions, regardless of the fact that one time I missed the majority of the semester with literally no reason whatsoever.

Before I go any further, let me explain my situation. My brother and I lost our dad early into our teens. Our mother raised us for the most part already, but after that, it was officially just the three of us. My mom worked nights as a restaurant manager, so as kids, we were alone often. This meant we could do practically whatever we wanted... and we did.

We weren't wild children, but we definitely took advantage of our mom all too often. We knew she would be there to wash our dishes, do our laundry, and clean the house, so we rarely cleaned up after ourselves. Of course, this became a habit.

By the time my wife and I shared our first home together, I was used to leaving a pile of dirty laundry on my floor, and leaving dishes wherever I finished eating. I actually remember, when I was about 14 years old, my mom saying, "if you could just take the dishes *near* the kitchen, instead of leaving them all over the house, that would help."

I probably don't need to tell you that my wife was not ok with my lifestyle, and she let me know quickly.

I still remember the day I asked my wife if she knew where a clean shirt was, and she pointed to the pile of clothes on my floor. I didn't have any clean shirts. I'm sure I just grabbed one off the pile and did the sniff test, but that moment really showed me how oblivious I was to my lack of discipline.

The next day, I was a disciplined machine, and I never struggled again. Right? Ha! This area was a strain on our marriage until I started to see the importance of my discipline, and the importance of changing my habits.

I started working on my discipline when I was in my early 20s, and it took years for me to see progress. It doesn't have to be like that. I didn't know anything about creating discipline, so it took me longer. Fortunately for you, you have this book that will lay out the steps plainly, based on my research and personal experience – my success and failure.

So what was the one area I mentioned earlier that I was actually disciplined in? Work. Seems weird, right? I had a great work ethic, because my mom instilled the importance of that in me. That's amazing, because it shows me that I can instill discipline traits in my kids and watch them come to fruition, as they [not so] slowly become adults.

She didn't instill other discipline in me, because she felt like she was serving me by doing everything at home for me. While I love my mom to death, I had to later explain to her how doing everything for us actually hurt us as adults. She understands now and fully supports my wife and I, and our quest to instill discipline into our own children.

Steps to Discipline

Strengthening your discipline muscle really can be compared to any other muscle. You've got to work it out. And the first step is to find an area of your life that needs it the most.

Step 1: Find a Discipline Catalyst

This is your discipline focus area. You need to find something you can use to strengthen that muscle, and it's not a bad idea to use an area you are really weak in. Many people use the gym—running or some other form of physical exercise—as their discipline catalyst. I chose finances.

When my wife and I got married, she had a pretty good idea of how to handle money. She had been through several finance classes and a few workbooks. I had not. I was too busy learning how to spend as much money as possible on a credit card without paying it off... and I had gotten pretty good at that. I knew the way I handled money was stressing her out, so I decided to use this as my first area to build discipline in.

Fast-forward a few years down the road, and we were completely debt-free. I say "we," but all of the debt was mine. I'll explain the rest of this story in chapter 7. I don't want to make it sound easy. It was a long, painful journey, but it was worth it. You've got to go through the steps though, which leads me to the next step, after you've found your discipline catalyst.

Step 2: Begin the Building Process

It's not a quick process. As Dave Ramsey would say, "we're in the business of crockpots, not microwaves." That doesn't mean it's going to take a decade, but you must be willing to give it enough time, whether it's finances, exercise, or anything else.

When I chose finances as my discipline catalyst, that meant a few things for me. First, I had to stop spending money on whatever I wanted whenever I wanted it – that good old American instant gratification. Then I had to stop eating out for every meal – I feel like there could be something here related to my being American as well. I also made the decision to cut up my credit cards and use cash for every purchase. And the final decision: I worked multiple jobs to pay off all the debt I had accumulated.

I want to point out one thing here: I chose finances for two reasons. First, because I knew I needed to change my spending habits or we were going to be living in a van down by the river, trying to spear fish, like Tom Hanks in *Cast Away*. I love *Cast Away*, but let's be honest, I would starve to death before I was able to spear a fish. Second, I chose finances as my discipline focus area because I had a good work ethic when it came to my job. I didn't do anything around the house, but I had a sense of pride in my job, and I was good at making extra money, because I was so good at working.

You may want to choose an area that really needs to be addressed out of necessity, but you also may want to look into an area you already have some discipline in.

Often, one area can have both of those qualities.

Step 3: Stay Dedicated to the Process

We all know discipline requires dedication, and that's really where the difficulty begins. Whether you read the studies that show habits take 21 days to form, or the studies that show habits take three months to form, you know it takes a while. We'll get into habits more in chapter 4, but this is a primer. Generally, the first 10 days are really tough, and you have to push through. The next 10 days are easier, but you know the habit isn't solid yet. The 10 days after that are the easiest, which lets you know you could really do this. So there you have it, wait at least 30 days before you can see the habit start to stick.

Honestly, even though it may seem hard, it's not that tough to get out of bed and go for a morning run. Once. It's building up your running habit and turning it into a regular thing that's difficult.

You must stay dedicated to the process.

This lesson really sunk in for me while I was in Basic Training for the United States Air Force. We were up well before 5:00am every day. Not five days a week, not every day except Sunday, but *every single day*. There was no going back to bed or taking naps. There was no doing your own thing or having personal time. You're on their time, all the time, for the entire time.

Looking back on it, Basic Training wasn't the hardest thing I've ever done, but it was tough, and it was tedious. I didn't come out of Basic as a disciplined machine (if only discipline was so simple), but it did strengthen my discipline in many areas. It taught me to stay dedicated. I saw the physical progress from the workouts. I saw the mental progress from the classroom. I saw the spiritual progress from staying consistent with prayer and fellowship at the chapel on Sundays. Basic Training taught me more about *myself* than anything, and that's really where I learned the value of consistency and dedication.

Now I'm disciplined in many areas of my life. I help my wife take care of the laundry and dishes, as well as our five children. Yes, I've finally learned how to help with the laundry and dishes, among other things, around the house.

I'm not telling you all of this to say I have everything figured out and my entire life is together; I'm telling you all of this to show you can be really terrible at this discipline stuff and still manage to change your habits and obtain self-discipline. I don't think anyone would have expected me to be where I am now if they knew me when I was younger.

That being said, I have learned one thing you don't do if you want to build discipline: don't do too much!

Step 4: Don't Go Overboard

If you study discipline, you'll find almost everyone agrees on this point. You don't want to try to build discipline in every area of your life at the same time. Want to start a new habit? Awesome! Want to start 20 at the same time? Why do you hate yourself?

Start with one area, and add one more area at a time. Slowly. Here are some common areas for discipline growth:

- **Finances** – Get out of debt, invest for retirement, create an emergency fund
- **Health** – Lose weight, gain strength, quit smoking, break an addiction
- **Marriage** – Spend more alone time with your spouse, take an extended vacation together, go on dates
- **Family** – Cut back at work, spend more quality family time together, get out and do more stuff together
- **Personal** – Read more books, increase prayer or meditation time, start a productive morning ritual

Some people may need to improve exact opposites. Brenda may need to stop being lazy and find extra work to pay off debt, while Donnie may need to cut back at work and focus more on family.

We're all different and our discipline can be built differently. If you try to build discipline in too many areas, your willpower will fail you. Just like discipline, willpower is like a muscle, which means fatigue sets in. They're almost the same muscle, but not quite. Discipline is about consistency over the long haul, while willpower is about each action you take. However, the energy to take action comes from the same place.

We've all seen the way people make changes in movies, and we try to replicate that. Here's how the typical movie goes:

The young man is picked on one time too many, so he decides he's going to get in shape, lose weight, get stronger, or whatever the role calls for. So the next morning, he's up four hours earlier than normal for an intense workout that sparks a series of intense workouts, until he's fighting like Rocky. Let's not forget that he completely changed his diet to accommodate his new exercise routine. Just like that. Diet, exercise, and sleep routine: completely transformed.

That's not real life. Here's real life:

The young man decides he wants to make a change, so his alarm goes off super early the next morning, he hits snooze a few times, and finally gets out of bed 30 minutes earlier than normal. He realizes he tried to change his routine by way too much, but he's still somewhat motivated, so he heads downstairs and puts on his running shoes. Five minutes into the workout, he realizes it's been two years since he ran more than 20 steps, and his body starts hurting. Everything starts hurting. He stops and starts walking... back to his house.

He gets back home and decides to try to keep this new routine going, so he makes a healthy breakfast. After eating some egg whites and broccoli, he realizes he's still hungry, since he did just run for the first time in two years. So he grabs the nearest box of Lucky Charms and has his way with it.

What happened there? Why did he seem to fail so badly and why does this sound so familiar? Because he tried to change too much at once, and he was out of willpower almost as soon as he started. Hopefully, this is really how the second story ended:

The young man realized he tried to change too much at

once, started to learn more about discipline and willpower, and began making smaller changes. His next morning consisted of a two-minute run. He slowly increased his run time over the course of the next three months until he could run a 5K without stopping.

Happy now? I know I feel better about his life. This example may be a bit extreme, but it's not far off of real life. Real people make decisions like that every day, because they were never properly taught how willpower works. You only have so much. While some new research suggests decision fatigue isn't a thing, there is a lot of evidence to support the idea of willpower depletion.[1]

It Gets Easier

"If you do not conquer self, you will be conquered by self."

— Napoleon Hill

Building discipline may seem difficult at first, but it's necessary for taking control of your life, and it does get easier. It seems like the older you are, the more difficult it is, which is probably where the phrase, "you can't teach an old dog new tricks," comes from. Of course, we know we can do anything we set our mind to, so that old adage doesn't bother us.

Just like pushups get easier as you train for them,

discipline in general gets easier as you continually do the work, over and over. Discipline is merely a choice to do something or not do something, whichever may be the right choice for you. The more you make the right choice, the easier it becomes to make that same choice. That's why the first day of a new workout is so hard.

If you don't control your life, your life will control you. Discipline makes the difference in the direction your life goes. And now for my favorite—and possibly the most important—part.

Discipline Begets Discipline

This is one of the most important takeaways from this chapter. Discipline is contagious and addictive. The more discipline you acquire, the more discipline you can expect to see in the near future, because building discipline brings on more discipline.

Making better eating choices will lead to a desire to do more exercise, or vice versa. Becoming healthier will lead to a desire to take better care of your body in other areas. Waking up earlier could easily lead to a desire to start making other positive changes in your life.

Yes, discipline begets discipline.

Maintenance mode is a lot easier than getting started. Once you push yourself to start something, and you see the change, you'll have no problem maintaining that success. That applies to any new habit, routine, or ritual you create. This is why getting started is so important, even if you don't feel like it. Even if you think you might fail, show up. Even if you think it's not possible, try it.

Every small increase will lead to another small increase, and that will snowball into an avalanche.

The problem is, this is also what keeps us from starting. We see the end game and how far it is, and that can suck the motivation out of us. It's easier to spend hours reading about losing weight than it is to put down the soda or candy that isn't helping you reach your goal. That's why starting a mediocre workout routine is better than spending hours finding the "best" one. You can always make adjustments to anything you start, but if you keep waiting until you find the perfect system, you'll be waiting forever.

In fact, the best thing you can do when you don't know what to do is *something*. Do something. Why? Because action cures fear. It's true. Taking action can eliminate fear, but we'll talk more about that in the next chapter.

Discipline and Passion

When I first started writing, I would wake up at 5:00am and write for an hour or longer... every day. That was two hours before I would normally wake up. I knew I needed to write in the mornings, because I didn't want my writing to take away from my family. I thought it was going to be a difficult transition, but it wasn't.

It wasn't difficult because I was passionate about what I was doing. I had been wanting to start a blog for years, and I was finally doing it. Quickly, I found a love for writing, so waking up wasn't much of a challenge.

Fast-forward a year down the road and I started to lose some of my passion... I found it harder and harder to get out of bed. It was depressing until I realized what was going on. Then I simply found a way to bring back my passion. I realized I had started to write about unfamiliar topics, and subjects that didn't interest me. I got back on track, and started writing about what I loved to write about again.

Magically, my discipline was restored, and I was up at 5:00am writing every day again. I had never been consistent with an early morning routine until I found something I was passionate about.

You can't expect to wake up early, and actually get out of bed, for no reason. Likewise, you can't expect to stay disciplined in doing something you hate. Discipline is not torture.

Applying Discipline Through Passion

How does this apply to you? What are you passionate about, and where are you trying to implement discipline? If you're trying to start a new running habit first thing in the morning, and you hate running (and mornings), it's not going to happen. Stop torturing yourself! Find a form of exercise you love to do, and do that.

You have to experiment to figure out what you're passionate about, but it's worth the time it takes. Don't spend years of your life thinking you're an undisciplined buffoon, only to figure out you were doing it to yourself this entire time.

This is common when we try to imitate others. Here are some examples:

- You have a fit friend who runs marathons, so you think you should start running marathons
- You meet someone who has acquired wealth through selling online, so you think you should do the same
- You know someone who is living in a home they can't afford and making it work, so you think you should follow suit

There's nothing you should do just because someone else is doing it. It may be your thing; it may not be. Don't assume that because someone else loves something, you'll love it too. You can always try it, but find what works for you. That's key in creating discipline.

Summary & Action

Discipline is built by doing the difficult things.

- *Do you take the easy way out?*

Discipline begets discipline.

- *Are you practicing discipline to build more discipline?*

Discipline is built more easily with passion.

- *What's something you're passionate about?*

Action: Discipline is best expressed through habits. The chapter on habits will dive deeper into how you can actually increase your discipline through the habits you create. Start something new today that will get you closer to your goals.

Reflection:

3

ACTION

Discipline never begins without action, so it would be easy to argue that action is more important. If you don't get started, you'll never do anything. Obvious, right? But it needs to be said, because millions of people are still waiting around to get started.

Let's talk about action.

This is the shortest chapter for a reason. You'll see why.

Action Cures Fear

The single greatest thing you can do for yourself is to take action. You don't have to get it right; you just have to get started. If you don't know what to do, and you take the first small step, the fear will slowly fade away. We're always afraid to do things we've never done before, but taking action reduces that fear.

Don't wait until you *want* to do something. You may be waiting forever. Do it now, because you know you need to. You may never want to. That's not the point. You may be afraid of taking the first step. Do it anyway. If you take action, you won't have time to be afraid. And the greatest thing happens when you take action: you start a motivation wave. That's right, you can create motivation – you can create a motivation wave.

Motivation Waves

You know what a motivation wave is, because you've experienced it before. Maybe that's not what you called it, but you'll soon see it's likely happened to you before. Think about that time when, out of nowhere, you decided to organize your entire DVD library. Or the time your house was messy for weeks until one day you decided to clean, and you cleaned the entire house before dinner. Those are motivation waves. They're real, and you must take advantage. In fact, you can create them. Sometimes they show up unannounced, and we don't know why, but you have to use them wisely. But the more important thing to know is that you can create motivation waves by taking action and getting stuff done.

Motivation always follows action.

Once you start to implement this on a regular basis, you will start to see huge results. You're essentially batching tasks together, and using action to create the motivation required to complete those tasks (we'll talk more about batching tasks in chapter 6).

The next time you have a couple hours free, make a list of things you need to do, and start acting on them. Watch how it gets easier and easier as you go through the list. The motivation will get stronger as you check off more items. It's not hard to get things done; it's only hard to get started.

This is a method of forced productivity. If you just start *doing*, your accomplishment will be motivating, and you'll want to do *more*. You could always boost the time by taking caffeine before you get started, for example, but only if you're working in the first part of the day. The caffeine and the motivation wave will keep you awake if you start too late.

This isn't all just a "good idea," it's an actual method that works. I have used this method over and over, and the motivation does come. And then riding a motivation wave feels so productive. There's no better way to get a large task, or a long list of small tasks, done. And there's no better way to spend a few free hours.

Sometimes the only thing you can do is take action, whether you want to or not, and you'll be surprised how it actually works.

Summary & Action

This is the shortest chapter for a reason.

- *Which areas of your life can you take action in today?*

Action cures fear.

- *Where can you take action to cure fear?*

You don't have to get it right; just get started.

- *Where can you get started today, even if it's a small step?*

Action: Take action today. Do the first step. Whatever it is that you want to do. Try being productive for the sake of being productive, and watch your motivation increase.

Reflection:

4

HABITS

> *"We are what we repeatedly do, excellence then is not an act, but a habit."*
>
> — ARISTOTLE

Your habits define you. You really are what you do repeatedly. If you write repeatedly, you're a writer. If you run repeatedly, you're a runner. If you lift weights repeatedly, you're a weight lifter. We're going to dive into all kinds of methods, tips, and techniques for building habits, but I think the most important technique has to do with your identity. So we'll start there.

Identity-Based Habits

If you want to make a change in your life—especially a

dramatic change—you have to change your identity in that area. What does that look like? It simply means you identify as someone who is the way you aspire to be. The idea is that you're becoming "the type of person who..." for whatever the action is. The end goal is to *become* that person, but the goal for today is to *identify* as that type of person.

"I'm the type of person who writes every day."

"I'm the type of person who runs 5x a week."

"I'm the type of person who reads for 30 minutes a day."

Fitness

- I'm a runner
- I'm an athlete
- I'm a weight lifter
- I work out regularly
- I never miss a workout

Personal

- I'm a writer
- I read daily
- I write daily
- I journal daily
- I never miss a day of writing or journaling

Business

- I'm an entrepreneur
- I promote my business daily
- I contribute to my business daily
- I'm a savvy businessman (or woman)
- I read for 30 minutes a day about my business

This is who you want to become, but first, you must *identify* yourself as that person.

How do you become this new identity? You simply follow through on the things you say you're going to do. If the identity is, "I'm the kind of person who never misses a workout," you have to make that true. If you never miss a workout, the details will come, but the identity-based habit has been formed.

This works best when you focus on a single area at a time. Trying to change several identities at once can be overwhelming.

Speaking of overwhelming... a brief word on your emotions.

Habits and Emotions

Contrary to what some of the old-school habit teaching says on creating habits, your emotions *are* one of the keys in habit building. The idea of building habits with pure discipline has been brought to trial, and it's not looking good for it. We all know self-discipline alone—though important and powerful—isn't enough to build a new habit, but then we keep trying to do it with self-discipline alone.

The connection between your emotions and building

new habits has been touched on, but nobody has covered it with such detail and accuracy as BJ Fogg, PhD, behavior scientist at Stanford University and author of the groundbreaking book, *Tiny Habits: The Small Changes That Change Everything*. Dr. Fogg explains the connection between celebrating and successful habit building. When you first hear of his tiny-habit method, this part may sound silly. Here's how the process works: You select a prompt (e.g., brushing your teeth), then you add the habit (e.g., two pushups), then you celebrate (e.g., saying "awesome," fist pumps, etc.).

I'll be the first to admit this idea sounded ridiculous. I could get on board with creating small habits, easily, but the celebrating usually got... left out. That is, until Dr. Fogg finished his book and explained the reason you're celebrating. You're training, or hacking, your brain to associate that action with success. Even something as simple as saying "awesome!" right after completing a habit will make the connection in your brain. This is a reward for completing the habit, and rewards have to be immediate or our brain won't make the connection. For example, you can go out to see a movie as a *reward* for hitting your gym goals, but your brain sees that as an *incentive*, not a reward.

Emotions play such a huge part in habit creation. Use that to your advantage. Go with your emotions when they're pushing you positively, but be mindful of them when they're working against you.

The Habit Process

Habits are created through repetition, and yes, to an extent, self-discipline. Discipline begets discipline, so it will create a snowball effect with your habits. But the best way to begin any new habit is to start small... so small it's laughable. If you want to do 100 pushups, start with one. If you want to run a marathon, start with running for one minute.

Of course, it depends on where you're at in any process, as far as *how* you should create a new habit, but the idea is to start easier than you can handle. This takes the fear and intimidation out of it. It actually makes habit-forming easy. This is how all consistent habits start. Think about bad habits for a minute. The alcoholic started with one drink. The smoker started with one cigarette. The gambling addict started by simply walking into a casino.

Add new habits gradually. One at a time. If you have time to add several habits, add a new, small habit each week, or month. This is a slow, but effective, way to build life-long habits. If you stumble, start where you left off, but keep going. What happens if you miss a day? Or a week? Or several weeks? You pick back up. You keep going. You're not a failure for missing one time. You only fail when you decide to quit entirely.

It's also good to have a standard rule of never missing more than two days in a row with anything. Missing one day happens, but when it comes to missing that second day in a row, you can find a way to make it happen and keep the habit going.

Here are the four steps to create a new habit, simplified:

1. Start small
2. Increase each day
3. Increase by small intervals
4. Continue building until you're satisfied

Then repeat the process with another new habit. It seems simple, because it is simple. It's not always easy, but the idea is easy, and you're more than capable of doing it. While it's easy to do, it's just as easy not to do. You can always create a new habit. You just have to start small enough.

Here are a few ways to start some popular habits:

- **Reading** - Read one page, or one minute, per day. Increase by that amount daily or weekly.
- **Pushups/Situps** - Do one pushup or situp, every other day. Increase by one each day.
- **Weight Lifting** - Start all lifts with the bar. Increase by five pounds each week.
- **Meditation** - Meditate for one minute per day. Each week, increase by one more minute each day.
- **Writing** - Write 100 words per day for a week. Each week, add 100 more words to your day.
- **Healthy Eating** - Track your meals. Eat only healthy meals one day per week. Increase by one day each week.
- **Prayer** - Pray for one topic a day. Add one topic each day.

The best way to stick with any of these habits is to incorporate them into your daily rituals. Rituals and repetition are both essential to your success.

Daily Rituals

You have about 25,000 mornings in your adult life. Make them count. The morning time is powerful. You should claim your mornings and not let your desire to get a few extra minutes of sleep dictate your morning flow. A lack of sleep likely isn't why you're tired anyway, but we'll get to that in the next chapter.

I have two personalities: my night-self and my morning-self. Sometimes we don't get along. When my night-self decides to stay up a little later, my morning-self pays for it. My night-self goes to sleep thinking about all the great and productive things I'm going to do in the morning. But sometimes my morning-self wakes up thinking my night-self is an over-achiever who doesn't focus enough on sleep.

Sound familiar? You have to learn how to combat your morning self.

Becoming a Morning Person

I decided I wanted to be a morning person. This is what happened the following morning: I woke up earlier than I ever had before, and I had the most productive morning of my entire life. So the next day I woke up and did it again, right? Nope.

I let my morning-self defeat me the following day. That's when I realized I have to learn how to deal with the morning me, by planning ahead the night before. I would wake up thinking about the mountain of tasks I planned to do the night before. It was intimidating.

Eventually, all of that changed, and I started waking up consistently and energetically. Every morning. It was actually pretty easy to make the transition when I used the right process.

Here are some things I started doing:

1. Sleeping 7.5 hours (minimum) each night
2. Drinking water as soon as I wake up
3. Having a ritual at night to wind down
4. Rewarding myself for waking up daily
5. Only drinking caffeine before noon

I know this is where most people would say something about the importance of breakfast, but I really don't think it's that important. Actually, if you eat a carb-heavy breakfast, it can decrease your productivity. I work better, and I'm more creative, when I'm slightly hungry. So I don't eat breakfast. I typically follow an intermittent-fasting window where I eat between 11:00am and 7:00pm. It's important to eat high-quality, real food. However, many studies are starting to show that *when* you eat makes little to no difference. I'm not a nutrition expert, but this is something to consider.

Perfect Your Mornings

I wasn't always a morning person. As you just saw, it is possible to become a morning person. You just have to take it one step at a time.

Here are some ways to deal with the morning you:

- **Commit to One Thing** – Commit to doing just one thing that gets you out of bed, like brushing your teeth or drinking a glass of water. After that, you can go right back to bed. However, once you're up and thinking clearly, you'll usually stay up.
- **Think About One Thing** – Stay in the "one-thing" mindset. As soon as you wake up, your mind is flooded with everything you have to do all day. That's not motivating for the morning you. Take it one step at a time. Give yourself time to wake up before piling on more.
- **Schedule a Nap for Later** – It's much easier to get out of bed when you know you can take a nap later on. Naps are actually used by some of the most productive people in history, including Winston Churchill, Thomas Edison, and John F. Kennedy. So don't feel lazy, it's productive!
- **Plan Your Mornings at Night** – You're more likely to wake up if you prepare the night before. Set out your clothes, set up your coffee for easy preparation, write your three MIT (Most Important Tasks) for the next day. Do whatever it takes for your morning to run seamlessly. A productive morning starts the night before.
- **Drink Some Water** – The morning is the most important time to hydrate your body, since

you go so long without water while you sleep, and water is the most important thing we put into our body. After drinking a large glass, you may not even need coffee.
- **Stop Hitting Snooze** – The snooze button is our first opportunity to practice discipline or procrastination each day. Don't start your day with procrastination. Once your morning self gets out of bed, you'll realize those nine minutes weren't worth it. Why not turn off your snooze option, or buy an alarm clock without a snooze?

Morning Rituals

Mornings are the best time of day to have a ritual. You're often alone, so your time isn't dictated by others, and you have the only say in what you need to do. Here are some things to try:

- **Affirmations** - This is part of the morning rituals of some of the most successful people in the world. The idea is to affirm something that is true about yourself, but it's also a good idea to affirm something you want to be true about yourself. Write these down and speak them out loud. If you're affirming something that isn't true yet, state it as if it's already true.

Example: *"I am a master of my finances. I am debt-free and financially-free to do the things I am passionate about with my life."*

- **Gratitude** - There's no better way to start the day than by saying thank you. Gratitude is a practice that will improve your life all around. If you're an optimist, this should be easy. If you're a pessimist, practicing gratitude is one of the quickest ways to become an optimist. We all have so much to be thankful for, so why not speak it and write it down?

Example: *"I am thankful for my health and the time I am able to spend with my family because of it."*

- **Silence** - Silent time can be for many different things. It's a great time for meditation or prayer. It's also a great time to sit and think. If you're used to rushing in the mornings, avoid the snooze button and wake up nine minutes earlier – use that time for silence. You'll be amazed at how smoothly your day goes just by adding a little silence and solitude.

Example: *A simple morning prayer will suffice. Or try meditating by focusing on one thing (i.e., your breathing).*

- **Exercise** - Get the blood pumping and get the health benefits. You'll feel better, look better, and live longer – exercise will also help you to actually wake up and conquer the rest of your morning. There's nothing like a quick morning workout to help you feel awake and alive. Remember, more sleep isn't always the answer when you're tired –

sometimes you just need a little exercise in your life.

Example: *Do the exercise you love. If you have the time, you can go for a walk, run, lift weights, or do bodyweight training. If you're rushed, try burst training, or HIIT (High Intensity Interval Training). Anything to get your blood pumping!*

- **Family** - The morning is a great time to relax and spend time with your family. Before the kids go to school, you can have a nice breakfast, or if you don't get a lot of alone time with your spouse, you can use the mornings to do exactly that – before the kids wake up. Starting your day with family time will set a positive tone for the rest of your day and improve your relationships at the same time.

Example: *Have a nice breakfast with the entire family, or just you and your spouse. You can also use the time to talk, read together, or do a couple/family devotional.*

- **Learning** - Read, watch educational videos, listen to audio teaching, or take a free online class. Whichever method of learning you prefer. If you just devote a few minutes to learning each morning, you'll be surprised how much you can accomplish in a month or a year.

Example: *Read for 20 minutes each morning, either in your field, or in a topic you want to learn more about.*

- **Journaling** - Journaling has been a common practice of many people throughout history, like Benjamin Franklin, for example. Journaling has many different forms. You can simply get a blank book and write, or you can get a structured journal. There are countless structured journals out now that walk you through daily journaling. Journals are great for personal use, and/or to leave to your children and family when you pass away.

Example: *Start with something you have around the house (e.g., journal, notepad, etc.). Once you build the habit of daily journaling, buy a nice journal, like an expensive, blank, leather-bound book, or a guided journal.*

- **Ritual** - The best way to maximize your productivity is to combine several of these into your own ritual. Find the ones you like the most and do them every morning. If you have time to do each for 10 or 15 minutes, that's great! But even if you can only devote a couple minutes to each one, it will add up over the long haul.

Example: *Start with combing a couple. You could try exercising and learning. After a couple weeks, add in another one. You can create more time for your morning ritual by waking up earlier, gradually, over a few weeks or months.*

Once you have a ritual, it will be easier to get out of bed. You'll look forward to your ritual every morning.

Perfect Your Evenings

Since the most important part of your morning is the evening before it, here are some ways to master your evenings:

- **Schedule Tomorrow** – I take this to the extreme and schedule each minute, but it simply means getting an idea of what tomorrow looks like. If you're a nerd like me and you want a literal itinerary, then go that route. If not, just write down what you need to get done, and the approximate times.
- **Your 3 MITs** – This is the most important thing to do (literally, MIT = Most Important Task), especially if you aren't already scheduling tomorrow the night before. Write down the three most important tasks you must accomplish tomorrow. When the morning hits, you'll know exactly what you need to get to work on.
- **Prepare Everything** – Set out the first clothes you'll need tomorrow morning. Prepare your water, coffee, or drink of choice. Set out your vitamins. Do everything you can to make your mornings easy.
- **Get Enough Sleep** – The next chapter is going to cover more on your energy. If you're not getting enough rest, your morning is going to

be unproductive, and so is the rest of your day.

Making it Work

It's a simple process to create habits, but it's difficult to stick with them. If you start small, and grow gradually, you *will* create positive habits. But you are the one who has to put in the work and the time. If you start big, you're setting yourself up for failure.

You know what to do, but it's on you to do it. It doesn't take much discipline to do a few pushups today, but it does take discipline to continue the habit.

Over time, your discipline will grow as the habit increases. We've already discussed discipline in chapter 2, but your daily habits are where that discipline truly comes into practice. Those habits create discipline.

Summary & Action

Identity-based habits are the most effective.

- *What or who do you identify as?*

Starting small ensures success.

- *Which areas of life can you scale down and start small... and how?*

Mornings are a great time to be productive.

- *What could your morning ritual look like tomorrow morning?*

Action: Start a new habit today. Something that gets you closer to your goals. Start so small you can't say no. Start with one habit; once it's built, add another.

Reflection:

5

ENERGY

Energy is the most important element of productivity, yet it's usually mentioned in a few sentences in productivity books, and then forgotten. It probably seems like I think every element in this book is the most important element of productivity, but the truth is, they all work together. You need all the elements, so in a way, they're equally "the most important."

Without energy, nothing gets done. Most of the time this gets dismissed by a simple, "of course, you need to get enough sleep, eat right, and exercise," or something along those lines. That's not enough. This is a vital aspect.

How can you use any productivity advice if you don't have the energy to get off the couch? I don't want to simply tell you what the problem is; I'm going to give you the solution...

Chris Bailey, from A Life of Productivity, conducted a year of productivity experiments. In his findings, he realized all of the productivity advice he consumed and wrote about, over the course of that year, could be categorized into three areas:

1. Time
2. Attention
3. Energy

Of course, we must have the time to do what needs to be done, and your level of attention is directly related to your level of energy.

Now that I have your time and attention (see what I did there?), let's dive in and see what you need to know about increasing your energy levels, because without energy, productivity advice is useless. We'll actually talk about sleep last, because I think it's overrated as the reason you're tired. Sometimes a lack of sleep is why you're tired, but *often*, it has nothing to do with it.

It's Not All About Sleep

Energy has less to do with sleep than you may think. Energy levels aren't merely derived from your sleep. Your energy has more to do with how you live your day.

New research suggests exercise can fight fatigue better than taking naps and sleeping more.[1] Naps are still a powerful tool, but exercise is more powerful. Exercise boosts your energy levels. If you wake up feeling tired, try going for a walk or doing some jumping jacks, then see how you feel. Trust me, it works.

In studies where groups have tried exercising versus not exercising when tired, the first group was shown to have more energy.[2] I think this sums up the typical thought process against exercising when tired...

"Too often we believe that a quick workout will leave us worn out — especially when we are already feeling fatigued," said researcher Tim Puetz, in a news release. Dr. Puetz recently completed his doctorate at the university and is the lead author of the study. He went on to say, "However, we have shown that regular exercise can actually go a long way in increasing feelings of energy — particularly in sedentary individuals."

Exercise is the key to more energy. But that's not all. Your diet is equally, if not more, important. Enough with the studies, research, and quotes from the docs... let's get into some practical ways to increase your energy:

1. Strategize your caffeine consumption, instead of overdoing it. Drinking a pot of coffee every morning is going to throw your caffeine tolerance through the roof. We're not trying to use caffeine as a crutch and become addicted, we're trying to use it correctly.
2. Exercise first thing in the morning, even if only for a few minutes. Get your blood pumping and you'll start to feel better immediately. Fight the first 15 minutes of fatigue. Do 20 pushups or 10 jumping jacks... burpees, anyone?
3. Drink lots of water, especially right after you wake up. Since we're mostly water and all, we need water... and lots of it. Drink at least half a liter of room temperature water immediately upon waking up.

4. Keep early morning meals light; think smoothies, fruit, and vegetables. Those are typically the best carbs to have in the morning. Or just go for a high-fat, low-carb meal, which will give you energy to get going, and keep you full until lunch.
5. Consume less heavy carbs (ex: white bread/flour, simple sugars, etc.). There's no good reason to consume junky carbs at all, but especially not in the morning.
6. Don't hit snooze. Those extra few minutes aren't real sleep anyways.
7. When all else fails, take a nap or tie this in with #1 and take a coffee nap. To take a coffee nap: make a cup of coffee, let it cool, and drink it quickly. Do this right before taking your nap, and you'll wake up 20 minutes later, full of energy. That is, unless you've killed your caffeine tolerance.

If you really want to take your productivity seriously and get stuff done, you need to work on increasing your energy levels. Sleep right, eat right, and exercise. That's really is what it's all about. Even if you work a desk job, you can still get up and take a walk every couple of hours. That will bring some energy back to your day.

Moreover, a green smoothie can give you the same boost as a cup of coffee. You can plan your meals in the most productive way possible, depending on when you are most productive. We'll talk about using your most productive times throughout the day, right after a mandatory message on how to sleep better.

Sleep Better

> *"When I woke up this morning my girlfriend asked me, 'Did you sleep good?' I said 'No, I made a few mistakes.'"*
>
> — STEVEN WRIGHT

If you're not getting a good night's sleep, you're not going to have a productive morning. I've got some tips for getting better sleep:

1. Avoid caffeine and alcohol within the last eight hours of your day.
2. Get a high-quality mattress and pillow. They make a difference.
3. Make sure the temperature is at a comfortable setting for you.
4. Avoid heavy meals at night. They decrease sleep quality.
5. Avoid "blue light" during the last few hours before bed.
6. Use visualizations when going to sleep. They are quite effective.
7. Use sleep tools, like black-out curtains and sleep monitors.
8. Sleep within sleep cycles, which means 90-minute increments.

9. Exercise regularly. People who do, sleep better.

Now that you know how to sleep, let's get back to your best time of day.

Your Best Time of the Day

Everyone is different. That's why there are night owls and morning people. Neither is right nor wrong, but you need to figure out which one you are.

We all have a time of day that works best for us. Some people have the most energy in the early mornings or nights, while others get the most out of the afternoon. Whenever it is, use that time.

Do some monitoring in your own life to see when you feel the best. You may feel more creative in the morning, but be more likely to do trivial tasks at night. Find the time to structure each task, according to how your body responds to that time of day. The bottom line, if you want to be productive, focus on your energy.

Summary & Action

Energy isn't just about sleep.

- *What can you change to increase your energy levels?*

Everyone performs best at a different time of day.

- *Which time of day is best for you?*

It's not all about sleep, but sleep is important.

- *Are you practicing proper sleeping habits?*

Action: Try something to increase your energy levels. If you're not sleeping well, it could be sleep-related, but it's best to find energy in other ways.

Reflection:

6

TIME

When I was stationed in Italy, I was busy. I was at one of the most active fighter bases in the world, and my schedule reflected exactly that. At one point, I found myself saying, "I just need more time." And then, all of a sudden, I had more time. I had an entire month. I knew it was coming, and I was looking forward to everything I was going to accomplish. All of the writing I would do, the progress I would make on my book, the gym time, the books I would read... all the things.

The month came and went. I didn't get much accomplished at all. I barely caught up on my writing. I missed the gym. I didn't finish reading a single book. I definitely didn't finish writing the book I was working on.

So what happened? Well, time isn't what I needed, and it's likely not what you need either. I needed to be more disciplined in my daily routine, and I definitely needed to stop procrastinatingly looking forward to some magical block of time in the future.

I was writing a little bit during the months leading up

to my month of free time, but for the most part, I was putting work off so I could batch it all together in that month. "I'll have plenty of time for that next month." Lies. I was telling myself lies. I was simply procrastinating.

The Procrastination Cycle

We would rather take advantage of a full Saturday morning than an extra 20 minutes before work. We always think tomorrow will be better because, "we'll have a little more time." This turns into a cycle of procrastination.

Our perception is not reality.

We don't see it that way. We think we have excellent time-management skills, because we're "going to get that done." And then a year down the road, we see little progress.

Discipline, Not Time

I'm not going to go back into discipline. We've covered that. But before we move on, it's important to realize your problem is likely not time; it's discipline. I had a month to get all kinds of work done, and I didn't. It was way too much time.

Taking a month-long *sabbatical* makes sense, because it's a month away from work. Taking a month just to work doesn't work. At least not for me. And not for most people.

Take writing, for example. Most of the famous writers, like Stephen King and Jack London, have used a daily word-count discipline to write all of their books. Occasionally you'll hear of writers like Elizabeth Gilbert, who takes long, concentrated periods of time to write her books, and doesn't generally keep a daily writing habit. But that's the exception, not the rule.

If you took an entire month, working 40 hours a week on your passion or side hustle, you still wouldn't put in as many hours as you can put in working 30 minutes a day for a year.

Small Batches

Batch-tasking is the act of grouping similar tasks into a specific block of time. You want to do all kinds of things that require "extra" time. Things like:

- Journaling
- Studying the Bible
- Reading a good book
- Meditating or praying more
- Writing your own book or blogging
- Hiking to a peak or running through your town

These are perfect things for your morning ritual. These are terrible things to batch into a large block of time, unless you're one of the few who works that way.

When I say *large block of time*, I'm talking weeks. Small batches work great. An extra two or four hours to devote to any of these things can be awesome and productive. Even an entire day can be nice, though that's on the line of being too much time. However, when you try to devote two weeks to any of these things, the time is overwhelming, you won't know where to start, and you'll waste a lot of that time. Moreover, just because a two-hour block of time is a great way to read your next book, that doesn't mean reading for 15 minutes a day won't get you to your goal faster; it likely will.

For all of these things you're trying to fit into your schedule, you need to be organized.

Classic To-Do Lists

Let me guess. You have a to-do list and you add to it every day. You promptly go through each item and check it off, one after another. By the end of the day, your list is completely empty and awaiting whatever tasks tomorrow holds.

Not so much?

Since you're here, reading this chapter (and since you're a human being), I'm going to assume it doesn't always go so smoothly. It doesn't go so smoothly for me either. It's more likely you're *constantly* adding to your list and *occasionally* checking something off.

Enough is enough. When your to-do list is so full you never see the bottom, it's time to change something.

Here's how to completely clear your to-do list and start getting stuff done, without overwhelming yourself...

Before You Clear the List

Keeping a clear head is a must, to be as productive as possible, so I suggest creating a brain-dump habit. This is a simple concept: have a place (physical or digital) to capture any idea that pops into your head at any time, and immediately get it out of your head.

I use an app that has a place for brain dumping. You can use anything from an app to a notepad, just get it out of your head. I have several different lists, including one I call "The Master List." This is the list I use to brain dump. If I hear of a new book, movie, or website I want to check out, I instantly put it on this list. If any idea pops into my head... it goes on this list. Then later, I'll come through and sort it into my "Reading List" or my "Idea List," and so on.

Now you know how my list is created. Your list may be similar, but let's talk about clearing it.

6 Steps to a Clear List

Here are the steps I take to clear my list. You can do this today, and I recommend doing it at least once per week from this point on. It may take several hours the first day, but after you do it once, you can do it weekly, and it will actually be a fairly quick process:

1. **Eliminate** – Go through every item on your to-do list and eliminate the unnecessary tasks. Some you've already completed, some may be outdated, and others may just not make sense anymore. Eliminate as many as you can.
2. **Automate** – You may have reoccurring tasks on your list (i.e., bills) that you don't have to be doing manually. Automate as much as possible and you will create time for other tasks. At a minimum, you can automate most

parts of your finances, but we'll talk about that in the next chapter.
3. **Delegate** – You have plenty of things on your list that need to be done, but that doesn't mean *you* have to do them all. Decide what you're willing to delegate and find the right person for the job. There are plenty of freelance websites to help.
4. **Postpone** – Many of the things on your list should simply be postponed. They may be important things, but there also may be so many more important things that you just can't do these right now. It's ok to postpone. It's ok to procrastinate when you're intentional.
5. **Breakdown** – Now you should have a list full of the top priorities and must-do items. Break them down into reasonable increments and small sessions. You're getting ready to start scheduling everything that's left – the magic happens in the schedule.
6. **Schedule** – Now that you have everything broken down, and you know about how much time you'll need for each, put everything into your schedule. Once it goes into your schedule, check it off your to-do list. You now have a time slot for everything.

Your schedule is the most important part. If you want to get things done, you must make time for things – you must schedule them. If you can't find time in your schedule for a task, you may need to put it off. You will also need to stick to your schedule for this to work. For substantial projects, schedule it daily.

For example: *If you're writing a book, figure out how many words or pages your book will be. Divide that number by the number of days you want to complete your book in. Then write that many pages or words each day.*

Once you put this stuff into your schedule, you'll be amazed at how it actually gets accomplished. To-do lists are awesome, but only when you actually do the things on the list. It can be stressful to feel like you're never going to clear your list. I hope you feel empowered to clear it now.

There's another important aspect here, and it's about how long things actually take you to accomplish. It's tough to make a schedule when you don't have accurate time slots.

We're about to get extremely practical. So practical it may seem silly, but it's important.

Measuring Time

Time is like money – if you don't tell it where to go, you won't know where it went until it's gone. And sometimes you won't even know where it went after it's gone. To really maximize your hours every day, you've got to know where your time goes, especially with the things you do day in and day out.

So before you start planning every minute and scheduling time for the most important things, you'll need to figure out where your time is going right now. Start by asking yourself these questions…

- How much time does it take you to brush your teeth and floss? You are flossing, right?
- How much time does it take you to shower?
- How much time does it take you to get dressed for work?
- How much time does it take you to drive to work?
- How much time does it take you to drive home? Is the traffic worse, better, or the same?
- How much time does it take you to eat breakfast? Lunch? Dinner?
- How much time does it take you to work out? Run? Lift weights?
- How much time does it take you to shop for groceries each week? Or month?

Perception of Time

The truth is, until you know how long these trivial, daily tasks take, you won't have an accurate idea of how much time you have for the high-priority items. We often have a false sense of how long it actually takes us to do things. That's why, "just give me five more minutes," rarely actually means five more minutes.

It may seem silly to time yourself completing these everyday happenings, but in the end, you'll be glad you did. You may even find an extra 15 or 30 minutes you didn't know you had. Until I timed my daily tasks, I didn't realize I had an extra 15 minutes each morning after getting ready for work. Now I use that time to read, which means I can read a couple extra books every month by using time I never knew I had.

Your life shouldn't be so robotic you develop an ulcer from all the stress of completing everything right on schedule. A schedule should be fluid, and ever-changing, with your daily rituals.

Just be careful. Figuring how long it takes you to do these things could lead to:

- Constantly being on time for work and meetings
- Newfound time to do the things you've been wanting to do
- More time with your significant other and/or children
- A calm, not rushed, feeling in the morning
- An extremely productive life

Knowing where your time goes is just as important as knowing where your money goes. This is like budgeting your time, or more like logging your time expenditures. Until we track our time, our time is easily stolen by the day.

Time Thieves

The average person spends nine years of their life watching TV, just from watching a few hours a day. But that's not you, right? I mean, you don't spend hours and hours in front of the TV. That's unproductive and a waste of your time... and you know it.

So what about social media? We spend an average of 144 minutes a day on social media. [1] Considering we spend more time than that on YouTube, it's hard to imagine there's any time left.

I think we all remember the first time we logged onto YouTube. Those suggested videos in the sidebar will get you... and keep you... for hours. As you will see in a moment, I used to waste hours every day, without even realizing it. You may be doing the same.

My High Horse

When my wife and I decided to cut our cable, we knew we were making the right choice. People acted like we were crazy. We heard a lot of..."You don't have cable?" and "Oh, I couldn't live without cable; I don't know how you do it."

We knew, since people were criticizing us, we were probably making the right choice. Because most people aren't doing the right things.

I felt proud of the fact that we were no longer wasting time in front of the TV. But as soon as I climbed atop my high horse, I immediately fell off and got kicked in the face... because after a few months, it dawned on me...

I replaced my tube time with a different tube... YouTube. And, of course, Facebook, and multiple other social media channels. Before I realized it, I was spending a couple hours each day watching videos and browsing my feed. I was on track to spend nine years of my life on my computer and my phone. Well that's not any better than TV, is it? With the number of stupid videos out there, I think it's worse.

So, here's what I did. It comes back around to tracking your time.

Track Your Media

I knew I needed the internet, because I had to blog, but that wasn't an excuse for me to waste my life, buried in my news feed.

I started tracking everything. Here's what I tracked

1. Television Time
2. Internet Time
3. Social Media Time
4. Video Game Time

Don't lie to yourself. It's really easy for us to try to justify the ways we waste time, so it's important to be honest. Sure, there are some educational videos out there, but for every informative and helpful video, there are a thousand useless videos.

Control Your Time

The good news is that you can change all of this. You may spend too much time on unproductive things, and that's normal, but once you replace them with productive things, you'll start to see some serious changes in your life.

Here are five tips to take control of your time:

1. **Time Yourself** – Seriously, use a timer and figure out how much time you spend on each type of media you engage in.
2. **Create Barriers** – Make it more difficult to do

the unproductive things. Delete apps or at least hide them.
3. **Plan Productivity** – If you plan productive things, you won't have as much time for useless things. Use a schedule!
4. **Plan Leisure** – Set aside a certain amount of time, that you determine, just for allowing yourself to be unproductive.
5. **Schedule Everything** – Schedule your days a week in advance. Make a plan and know what's going on each day.

It's fine to relax, but these time-wasters aren't always as relaxing as you may think, and you need to know exactly how much time they are stealing. The more productive you are, the better you feel. In the words of Ron Burgundy, it's science. Accomplishing tasks and goals releases endorphins that make you happy, which leads to more accomplishment.

Don't feel guilty. If you don't like the way you spend your time, simply change it. You'll be surprised how much you can accomplish when you cut the time-wasters. Once you understand where your time is going, and how much time you spend on each thing, you can implement some productive concepts.

Productivity Strategies

You want to work smarter, not harder. You want to be more efficient – more productive. What are some practical and applicable strategies and techniques that can help you do that?

1. Pareto Principle

Pareto Principle – *The 80/20 rule, which states that roughly 80% of the effects come from 20% of the causes, or 80% of the results come from 20% of the work.*

Think about it. In your daily life, where do results come from? Asking this question will help you determine where to invest your time. This goes for your personal and business life. Exercise, dieting, and personal development are a few examples. This rule really shows you how you don't have to be perfect, you just have to focus on what's important.

Put this into action: *Write down the top three most productive things in your work and personal life. Try to put at least 80% of your focus on the top 20% of the items and watch the results roll in. You may find that you're spending 80% of your time on things that really don't matter – things that are only getting you 20% of the results.*

2. Parkinson's Law

Parkinson's Law – *An adage that work expands so as to fill the time available for its completion. In other words, if you plan a one-hour block for a task, you will work at a pace that gets the task done in an hour.*

If I plan to write an article in two days, I will write it in two days. If I plan for 90 minutes, I'll get it done in 90 minutes. This is one of those crazy laws of life that just seems to work. Use it to your advantage. Most importantly, if you know you can finish something within a given time period, stop wasting your time and stop dragging it out.

Put this into action: *Use an actual timer and start setting some limits. Set a time to begin and a time to stop working.*

3. Pomodoro Technique

Pomodoro Technique – *The process of breaking your work into chunks. 25 minutes of work, followed by a 5-minute break – that's one pomodoro. Once you complete four pomodoros, take a longer break (20-30 minutes).*

Parkinson's Law is in full force with the Pomodoro Technique. Before long, you'll know what you're capable of during one 25-minute pomodoro, and you'll start knocking things out.

Put this into action: *Get a timer and start the clock. Work for 25 minutes, rest for five. After four pomodoros, take a 30-minute break. Then repeat the process.*

4. Eisenhower Matrix

> *"What is important is seldom urgent and what is urgent is seldom important."*
>
> — Dwight Eisenhower

I've heard this strategy referred to as many different things, and countless authors have used it in their books, but it's most commonly referred to as the Eisenhower Matrix. It's simple, but it requires you to be honest about your tasks, which is not always easy. You'll separate everything you need to do for the day into four categories:

- **Urgent and important** (do these immediately)
- **Important, but not urgent** (create your plan to do these)
- **Urgent, but not important** (delegate or automate these)
- **Neither urgent nor important** (eliminate these)

The problem is, we tend to focus too much of our time on the "urgent, but not important" and too little of our time on the "important, but not urgent." That's completely backward. Often, the "important, but not urgent" things are going to produce the greatest results in your life.

If something is important, but not urgent, that means, 1) it could be one of the most important things you'll ever do, and 2) it's easy to keep putting it off.

Put this into action: *Create your own box. It doesn't need to be fancy; a simple paper-and-pen box will do. Write down a list of everything you need to do (or could do) today. Put each item in its place. Then follow the action in the parenthesis above for each item (i.e., do urgent and important tasks immediately, eliminate tasks that are neither urgent nor important, etc.).*

There are so many productivity strategies out there, but these are the four most useful in my experience.

Here's another one that deserves a longer explanation: impose limitations. I'll explain...

Limit Yourself

So now that your to-do list is in order, you know where your time is going, and you're using strategies to maximize how you use it, ask yourself a few questions...

What's the point of productivity apps, to-do lists, and all of these strategies? Why does an article about "10 quick productivity hacks" catch your attention so easily?

The answer is simple: freedom. You want freedom.

But here's the interesting part: if you want more freedom in your life, first, *you must limit yourself*. Increasing your productivity is awesome. I write about it often, but it's important to increase your productivity in the right areas. You may be spending hours making something more efficient, when in reality, it should just be eliminated.

Tools, apps, and hacks are great for working smarter and getting organized, but first, figure out what needs to go. Then you can start using the tools to make yourself more productive with what's left.

WHAT YOU NEED IN LIFE

Efficacy – *The ability to produce a desired or intended result.*

What's truly important to you? Family? Relationships? Your business? Leaving an inheritance? A legacy? That's your starting point. Are you working hard towards things that aren't important? You may be. We've all been guilty of it.

Limiting yourself starts with limiting distractions. What are your distractions? We've talked about TV, internet, social media, and video games. Do you have more distractions?

True productivity means accomplishing what you've set out to accomplish. That's efficacy. Playing video games for a couple hours on a day you've set aside to play video games for a couple of hours is actually... productive. But that can't be every day.

Your Top ~~20~~ 10

Think of a quick list of the top 20 most important things in your life. Put them in order of most to least important. How important are the last 10 things? Are they even necessary?

In my list, I would include my relationship with Jesus, spending time with my family, my commitment to the military, exercise, and writing. That's my top five. The next five may include some important things like reading and traveling, but I can assure you the last 10 items would need to go.

How much can you cut out, and how much more time would that give you to focus on your top 10? Saying no to things is every bit, if not more important, than saying yes.

What to Cut

Personally, I know I could spend less time scrolling my news feed and I have. I've trimmed my life down to the bare bones and I keep trimming away. We should always be striving to become more productive in these areas.

How do you decide what to cut out? Simple, just ask yourself if it's getting you closer to your goals on the top 10 items. If it is, keep doing it. If it's not, cut it out.

Back to the video-game example. Playing video games with my kids on a Saturday morning gets me closer to my family goals. Playing video games by myself for 15 or 20 hours a week gets me farther away from my family goals. Therefore, I don't have time for the latter.

Freedom Through Limitation

If you want freedom, you must limit yourself. Overindulgence is not the answer. I could try to explain freedom through limitation and the importance of it all day, but instead, I'll save your time and use an example to sum it all up. Here's how this works...

Cheat days are a great example and they work for almost everything. The most common use for cheat days is within a diet, but the concept can also work for other things you typically overindulge in, like technology. How? Give yourself one day each week to overdo it. Eat whatever you want, watch TV all day, play video games from morning until midnight if you want.

But here's the kicker: you have to stay disciplined for the rest of the week. A cheat day on a diet won't be effective if you're cheating throughout the week as well. Once you get this down, it's extremely freeing. The food will taste better, the games will be more exciting, and you'll still be striving for your goals.

The best part? You won't feel guilty for doing it.

I remember the first cheat day I gave myself when I started the *Body for Life* program (which helped me lose 50lbs of fat). It was a good day. I ate everything I had wanted to eat all week. It felt great knowing I was still climbing towards my weight-loss goals, as I was eating half of a deep-dish pepperoni pizza. And after an entire day of it, I was ready to not look at unhealthy foods for another week.

If you want to put this into action today, start with a cheat day in some area. See how freeing it is, and then branch out to the rest of your life. Adding discipline into your life will only give you more freedom. Limits allow for freedom – the freedom to live your life to the fullest.

When we overindulge on a daily basis, we feel terrible (mentally and physically). We feel guilty, and we often feel sorry for ourselves. We don't even enjoy the things we continuously overindulge in. Moderation and limitation bring the enjoyment back.

If you want to feel better and be happier, set some limitations. You'll thank yourself.

Focus on What Matters

Opportunity Cost – *The loss of other alternatives when one alternative is chosen.*

We are always trading our time for something. Everything we do is a trade-off. It's called opportunity cost. If you want to be happy, accomplish your goals, and live a fulfilled life, you'll have to stop focusing on what doesn't matter and start focusing on what does.

How do you do that? You've got to take your time back.

There are small areas of your life that can make a huge difference. Let's get back to the practical. Start by spending less time on these things.

These are five freedom formulas:

1. Spend less time on what you wear

Create an easier method for getting dressed, like eliminating things in your wardrobe that don't match. This way you'll know you can wear any shirt, shoes, and pants together. Or you could go even more minimal and use a method like Barack Obama's idea to only wear blue and grey suits. Focus your time and energy on more important things. It's becoming more common for people to wear the same thing every day to eliminate one more daily decision. You don't have to go that far, but you get the idea.

2. Spend less time on what you eat

Separate your meals into two categories: meals for fuel and meals for pleasure. Instead of using those valuable morning brain cells (some of us only have so many in the morning) to decide what you'll have for breakfast, simply have the same thing every day or plan your meals ahead of time. Figure out which meals are truly for pleasure, such as dinner with the family or eating out with friends, and use those meals to carefully decide what you'll eat. For the other meals, don't waste time on them.

3. Spend Less Time Accommodating Others

This goes back to learning how to say "no." Don't spend your days constantly accommodating the needs of other people. Caring about others is important; however, being a people-pleaser can steal your time. You can apply this in several ways, such as avoiding unknown phone calls, and only checking email once or twice a day. Unknown calls steal your time and break your focus, and they are almost always unimportant (if they're important, they'll leave a message). Checking your email constantly can be extremely distracting, and most of the items in your inbox are for someone else's agenda. Put others on your time.

4. Spend Less Time Complaining

We all know complaining doesn't help anything, yet we all do it at one point or another. Not only does complaining not help, but it actually shifts you into a negative mindset and kills your focus. Try a 30-day no-complaint challenge. Simply go 30 days without complaining about a single thing and watch the results. When you're forced to practice optimism in every situation, you'll be surprised at how much better things go. You'll have ideas you would've never had if you were complaining – you'll be forced to look for solutions and change situations, instead of complaining about how bad they are.

5. Spend Less Time Regretting

We've all missed opportunities. If you make a mistake and learn from it, it's no longer a mistake; it's a growing experience with a lesson. Look back on anything you're not happy with. Make up your mind to take a lesson away from whatever it is, and then forget about it. It's over. It already happened and it can't be changed. Now that you're no longer complaining, it only makes sense to stop regretting. If you eliminate the time you spend regretting, you'll force yourself to be future-minded instead of living in the past. You'll reap some awesome benefits when you're living in the present and looking to the future. The past is over, so get over it.

Here's the bottom line: eliminate trivial choices so you can spend more time making decisions about things that matter.

Now for the final step to controlling your time: a weekly review.

The Weekly Review

You don't want a weekly review that takes several hours to complete. Because you won't do it. The good news is, a weekly review doesn't have to take several hours, but it can save you several hours throughout the week.

Here's a quick weekly review that doesn't take all day:

1. Clear

Clear your work area. This includes your physical desk and your virtual desktop. File or shred all the loose papers and close all the unneeded windows on your computer.

Clear your inbox. Inbox-zero is a good goal, but don't obsess over it. When I clear my inbox, I file it into three categories:

1. **Action Required** – If there is action to be taken on the email
2. **Reference** – For non-action emails I may need information from
3. **Archives** – Everything else

If you need to find an email, do a quick search. This will eliminate all the time spent filing. Searching has actually been shown to be quicker than looking for a filed email, according to a study by IBM Research. [2]

Clear your head. It's time for your brain dump. If you haven't already captured everything in your head, do so now.

2. REFLECT

Review the previous week. Figure out what went right and what went wrong. The good and the bad – you can learn from all of it. Come up with a list of questions to ask yourself like, "What did I do well? And not so well?" and "Did I reach my goals?". These are just examples, but they're great starting points.

Review the specific hours you spent. Did you spend more or less time reading than you wanted to? What about working on your side project? Journaling? Exercising? This will really highlight when you've been putting something off for a long time. It only takes a few weekly reviews to realize you're never going to get to some things unless you start putting them in your schedule now.

Review your "someday, maybe" list. If you don't have a "someday, maybe list," you should start one. It's one of David Allen's ideas that stuck with me, from his book, *Getting Things Done: The Art of Stress-Free Productivity*. You know all of those big dreams and ideas you have, like learning a new language, learning martial arts, or going skydiving? All the things you've always wanted to do, but can't right now. You're never going to actually do any of that if you don't write it down somewhere to remind yourself you want to do it. Just don't forget to actually review this list each week too.

3. Plan

Schedule your to-do list. Make sure everything that's done is checked off, and look at what isn't done. Once it's down to only things you haven't yet completed, you're ready to schedule. Remember, the only way you're really going to clear your to-do list is to schedule what's on it.

Schedule your upcoming week. Schedule everything. I schedule time for work, writing, and exercise, but I also schedule time for family, reading, journaling, and personal hobbies. I even schedule when I'm going to run errands based on where I'll be throughout the week.

Learn to be flexible. Sometimes you have to say "no" to people when you already have things on your schedule. It's important to stick to your schedule; however, you don't want to become a Time Nazi. It's ok to break away from your schedule occasionally, but don't make it a habit. I do my weekly review on Sunday evenings. It doesn't matter *when* you do it, only *that* you do it.

Pro Tip: *One thing that's helped me with my to-do list is adding a "next action" beside each item. This makes it super easy to schedule. If you have a large project on your to-do list, simply ask, "what's the next action that needs to happen for this item?". It may be as simple as doing some internet research. If that's the case, schedule that internet research. This is a sure way to be productive and clear your to-do list.*

The most important thing is to make this review process so easy you'll actually do it. Mine takes about 30 minutes, and never more than one hour. That's less than one hour for an entire week. One hour of planning can add up to 10 hours of productivity to your week. Planning is powerful.

∼

Summary & Action

Time isn't the problem; it's how you use that time.

- *Do you still think you need more time?*

Batch tasking works best in small batches.

- *What are some things you could batch task and schedule?*

If you want freedom, limit yourself.

- *In what ways can you limit yourself to gain more freedom in life?*

Action: Create a schedule. Take everything off your to-do list. Clear it today, and put it into a schedule. Start batch tasking things that are best done in chunks.

Reflection:

7

WEALTH

I was a financial loser. The average person knows little about finances, but somehow I feel like I knew less than that. We were $24,000 in consumer debt. We had no emergency fund, no investments, and no savings whatsoever. I had used most of my wife's savings to buy a new drum set (because that's what responsible husbands do).

I say *I was a financial loser*, because it really was just me. My wife had been through Dave Ramsey's course, *Financial Peace University,* and honestly, she knew much more than I did about managing money... and literally everything else related to money. She gave her input, but why would I listen? I was in my early 20s and I already had everything figured out. I didn't need her input – I knew what I was doing.

Yeah...

Eventually, my wife grew tired of our family always being broke (because of me), so she handed off the finances... to me. Scary, right? That's when I realized my spending was out of control and I had to make a change.

A couple hundred finance books (literally), and a BA in Finance later, I've got an understanding. I may have gone a bit overboard, but that's how far I've come and how bad it was.

I'm not going to drown you in the tears of my past wrongdoings, but I am going to tell you why you need to take control of your finances, what happens if you don't (from personal experience), and how to take control right now.

Yes, today is the day you will take control of your finances. Today is the day you will change the course of your financial life. Sound corny? Sometimes the truth is corny, but you *can* change your financial future if you start today. Let's do this...

Why Take Control?

I assume you want to take control of your finances and you don't really need a "why," but if you still want one, there are many. Taking control of your money doesn't mean being greedy or selfish. It's actually quite the opposite. The thing is...

Money controls your life more when you don't have it than when you do.

Here's why you've got to get control of your money:

- **If you don't control your money, your money will control you.** That's the simple truth. Someone or something is in control of your money right now. If you don't feel like it's you, it's probably your money. You may be a slave to your money without even realizing it.

- **Money is a great servant and a terrible master.** Money shouldn't run your life; money is there to make sure you're able to run your own life. If you have it backward, you'll spend your entire life a slave.
- **Nobody is going to do this for you.** Despite what a broker, money manager, or anyone else in a suit with a red power tie tells you, you have to do this for yourself. Sure, money managers can help with investments, but you need to have your finances in order before you trust someone else with your money.

If You Don't Take Control

Initially, if you don't take control of your money, you know what happens? Absolutely nothing. It's not like some huge alarm goes off that forces you to take control. It's a trickle effect over years and years… and it takes about that long to get your finances back on track if you let them go. If you blow your budget one month, you're likely to see no change in your overall financial situation. If you consistently blow your budget every single month, you'll find yourself in some serious financial heartache over the coming years.

Don't tell yourself you'll take control later. This is a big one. The old "well I guess I'll start next year" syndrome can cripple your finances. You've got to start this now – preferably today. Think about how many times you told yourself you were going to do something about it and you didn't. I promise, if you start today and take the advice I'm going to give you in this chapter, you will control your finances, but if you never get started, it can never happen.

Now I know you're really here for the "how." You're ready to do this and you want to get to it already. So how do you get started? It's easy in practice, but it can be difficult in discipline. You've got to stay disciplined. I'll explain why it doesn't even take much discipline, but you've got to stick with it. Can you promise me right now you will stick with this? This is for you and your family. Here's how you start...

How to Take Control

I first decided to take control of my finances because I was angry. I realized our finances were controlling the direction of our family. We couldn't do the things we wanted to do, because our finances were holding us back. Then one day, it really hit me...

I had finally decided to fulfill my life-long goal of joining the United States Air Force. I walked into the recruiter's office and explained how it had been a dream of mine, and how I was ready to do it. My smile quickly faded as I found out why I couldn't join. Well, for one, I was too fat, but that's a separate topic. Second, we were too broke – more specifically, our debt-to-income ratio was too high for the Air Force's standards.

That day pretty much did it, and this was right after my wife handed over the finances. The process began. First, I started listening to my wife (husbands, this is one of the best decisions you will ever make – they are smarter than we are – surely that's been scientifically proven by now). Second, I started reading every book I could find on personal finances. Third, I started working out to become... not fat. Two years later, we were completely debt-free, and I had lost 50lbs. I met all the standards and signed the papers to join.

That's my story. Now let's talk about yours.

Here are the five steps you need to take to get your finances in order:

1. **Track your spending** – The most important part of getting financially fit is knowing where your money is going. How can we be good stewards of our money and expect to be blessed financially if we don't know where it's going?
2. **Automate your finances** – Start now. Write down every reoccurring expense (e.g., bills, payments, giving, savings, investments, etc.). Now you'll begin the automation process. Bills can generally be automated through online banking. Physical checks (such as a rent check) can be automated through online banking as well, by setting a reoccurring check to be paid to a specific person or company. Investments can usually be set up for automatic withdrawal through your investment company, employer, or bank. Giving can often be automated through the church or organization you give to – if not, you can send the check through online banking automatically.
3. **Set your budget** – Now that your reoccurring expenses are automatic, you're just down to

budgeting your other expenses. Set a budget immediately and then adjust based on what you notice while tracking your spending. Cut out the things that are costing you too much and the things you don't need, then go from there.

4. **Eliminate your debt** – Before you move on to the final step, you'll want to eliminate your debt. At a minimum, you need to eliminate your high-interest consumer debt. Mortgages, student loans, or other low interest rates don't need to be eliminated before the fifth step, but you need to have a plan in place to pay as little interest as possible. For example, after you eliminate your consumer debt, you can cut down the usual 10-year term length on your student loans, and often, lower your interest rate by consolidating loans. It's simply a numbers game. It doesn't make sense to invest with an 8% return, while you're paying 27% on your consumer debt.

5. **Create wealth** – If your employer offers a match in your retirement account, invest enough to get the match. That's free money – a 100% ROI (return on investment)! And you should be investing that money, whether you're paying off debt or not (unless you're paying over 100% interest on one of your debts, and in that case, you got a raw deal). Once all your high-interest debt is paid off, you're ready to start some serious wealth

building. We'll talk about what that looks like below.

Those are the five quick steps to take control. Now let's elaborate.

Real-Life Budgeting

Budgeting is weird, because almost every financial guru recommends doing it, and almost everyone who tries to do it struggles with it. The truth is, there are a lot of things left unsaid when it comes to budgeting. There's a reason it doesn't work, or doesn't seem to work.

I'm going to explain how to actually budget effectively and cover some unanswered questions.

Zero-sum budgeting is the best way to budget, because it requires you to spend every cent on paper before you actually spend it. And that's awesome, because spending money is easy to do.

Here's how it works:

- **Get a spending plan form or use a digital tool.** Input all of your categories that can be automated. This can be as simple as a plain sheet of paper with your budget items jotted down.
- **Fill out the remaining categories that can't be automated.** The remaining should be things like groceries, entertainment, clothing, etc.. Take your best guess at how much you'll spend in each category.

- **Track your spending.** Download an app or get out a notepad.

Once you automate all of your static, reoccurring expenses, you're really only worried about tracking the rest of it. I've chiseled my budget down to five categories: groceries, dining out, other entertainment, auto, and clothing. Everything else (investments, savings, insurance, tithe/giving, and mortgage) is automated. I still include them in my spending plan so I don't forget about them, but those areas are already filled in. That means I only actually manage about $1,500/month. Everything else is automatic.

Why Budgets Fail

Normal people give up on their careers and their marriages, so it's not surprising they give up on their budget. Don't be normal. But most of the reasons people give up are reasons you can avoid.

Here are the most common reasons budgets fail:

1. **It doesn't seem to work** – Here's the deal, it's not going to work if you're new at budgeting. Budgets never work the first month, or the second. Often it takes multiple months for budgets to be effective, but it's worth the wait.
2. **Not planning the specific month** – There are different expenses for different months. If you'll be attending a birthday party, you'll probably want to buy a gift. If it's time to renew your license or your vehicle tags,

include that. Each month has its own specific expenses.
3. **Getting off track and just quitting** – You'll get off track. You'll forget to put some expenses in. That's perfectly fine, as long as you pick up where you left off and keep going. Missing a week or a month doesn't mean you have to quit.
4. **Striving for perfection** – Your budget will never be perfect. Trying to make it perfect and track every single cent is fine, until you start getting discouraged if it doesn't work out. There will always be missed money here and there.

Don't give up or get discouraged. Everyone struggles with this and no budget is perfect.

The most important thing you can do for your money is track it. Even if you completely stop every other part of your budget, tracking will keep you on... track. At least you'll know, by looking back, that you went way over-budget. In fact, if you don't want to budget at all, at least track each purchase so you can better gauge the amount you're spending. Tracking can be quite an eye-opener for most people.

Good budgeting is boring. Like I mentioned earlier, I only manage a small amount each month. The rest of my money is building my retirement, funding my children's education, giving to my church, and paying other bills. All of those things will happen automatically. In fact, if I just lived each month by taking out $1,500 in cash and spending until it was gone, I would still accomplish my major financial goals.

Budgeting gives you the ability to see patterns and adjust amounts based on what you spend and what you need to spend.

Why I Budget

I admit it. I don't follow every part of my budget, precisely, every month. I've fallen off the budget train many times, but I've always hopped back on. I don't budget to invest more, save more, or spend less, though it does allow me to do all of those things…

I budget for the sake of freedom.

I know I can buy everything in my budget, when I spend every cent on paper before the month starts. That means I never feel guilty about spending $50 to $200 a month on myself, as part of my "blow fund." I don't feel guilty about buying a new shirt when I have a clothing fund. I don't feel guilty when I'm eating out, because I know my limits, according to my budget.

Most of all, I never wonder if I spent more than I earned, because I spend everything on paper first.

I also budget because I recognize there are three costs associated with every purchase:

1. **Actual Cost** – The amount you actually pay (i.e., $3 for a cup of coffee).
2. **Opportunity Cost** – What you gave up by buying something (i.e., $3 invested for retirement).
3. **Hidden Cost** – The potential return you could

have earned. (i.e., $3 invested over 40 years, with an 8% return, is $65.17). I hope that $65 cup of coffee was good.

To me, this shows just how important it is to save a few bucks here and there on small things, because small wins can become big wins when compound interest is involved. I'm not saying you shouldn't buy that cup of coffee. I'm saying your small purchases matter more than you think.

I'm a finance nerd, so it's hard to justify not budgeting when I see how much of a difference a $3 purchase can make, but you may feel differently. You may hate budgeting. If so, welcome to the majority! Here's the good news for you: after all of this talk on budgeting, you technically don't have to do it. I'll explain...

Why You Don't Have to Budget

You can be successful without ever setting a budget by taking care of the important matters first, and then spending the rest.

Of course, you can't spend money you don't have, or you'll go into debt, and you could ruin everything. So if you take this approach, I suggest pulling out your monthly spending in cash, like I mentioned above, so you'll know when you're out of money. You could call this the Minimal Money Management system, or, you really don't have to call it anything. You plan enough on the front, so you don't have to worry about the back.

What are the important matters? Well, aside from paying off all your debt and having a fully-funded emergency fund (3-6 months of living expenses), [1] there are a few things you need to take care of.

If you set these things to automatically come off the top of your budget, you can freely spend the rest of your money on whatever you want... yes, you can buy that nice jacket or those yard gnomes you've been eyeing, but once you're out of money for the month, you still have to stop spending. So make sure you can pay for things like food and fuel before you get too attached to those adorable little yard gnomes.

Once you've automated the important things, here's the foundation that allows you to spend the rest. Make sure you're doing these things first:

- **Invest 15% for retirement** – After your debt is paid off and your emergency fund is fully funded, set up an automatic draft for 15% of your paycheck to go into retirement investing. We'll talk more about investing soon. You may want to do more than 15%.
- **Life Insurance** – Buy the appropriate type and amount of life insurance. Remember, life insurance is to replace *your income* for people who depend on it. It's for them, not for you. If you don't have anyone depending on you financially, you may not need it.
- **Other Insurance** – Hold enough health, auto, and home insurance to cover things you can't afford to replace (including your health). If you have assets, consider an umbrella insurance policy. If you rent, consider renter's insurance.

- **Create a will** – It's important to know what's going to happen after you die. If you have stuff, you need a will. It will make a difficult time in your family's life that much easier.
- **Save for large purchases** – There are always large purchases in the future. You may need a new-to-you car, or a down-payment for a home, in the future. Whatever it is, save an amount every month for this. If you don't need the money for at least five years, use the investing strategy below. If you need it before that, go with bonds or a money market account. The important thing is to save.
- **Give 10%** – This is optional, but I truly believe giving is the foundation of receiving, and your finances will never be fully blessed without this piece of the puzzle. Give to your local church or your favorite charity – the important thing is that you give.

If you have all those areas covered, you'll be financially successful. Even without a budget.

The bottom line: pay yourself and make sure you're protected first, then spend the rest. I would argue you'll be more prosperous if you include a budget in your planning, but if it stresses you out, it's not worth it. After all, budgets aren't for everyone.

Now let's get into the fun stuff: growing your money.

Investing Made Simple

There are few topics with as much contrasting information as investing. That alone is enough to scare most people away altogether. Is it really that difficult? Do you really need to devote years of your life to studying the most efficient way to invest? Do you have to know the ins and outs of the stock market? Do you need complex investing strategies just to beat inflation? It seems that way, right? But I'll make this simple: the answer to all of those questions is a resounding NO!

The problem with most investing advice is that someone is profiting (or attempting to profit) from it. When you read a book, they may try to sell you their system. When you read an article, they want you to invest through their affiliates. When your brother-in-law corners you after Christmas dinner, he wants you to invest in his company. I don't have a system for sale. You already bought my book. I'm going to tell you straight.

Investing is actually much easier to understand than it seems. You're about to learn everything you need to know to be a successful investor, and you may be surprised at how easy it is.

"Hot Stock Tips"

Turn on any business show; you'll see people blabbing about hot stock picks and attempting to explain the method to their madness. I can assure you, it's mostly just madness, with some greed sprinkled on top, but not much method (at least not one that works).

The vast majority of people in the world are terrible

at picking stocks. You probably are too. I'm not great at it. People like Peter Lynch and Warren Buffett are famous for a reason: they are some of the few who can consistently pick winning stocks. Yet, even they have their failures.

So should we just give up on the stock market? Absolutely not! It's the most efficient way to invest for your retirement. Other avenues, such as real estate and businesses, can be a great part of your retirement portfolio, but the easiest way to invest is through the stock market. All of those other investments are just icing on the cake.

However, picking *individual stocks* isn't the answer. Unless you're willing to devote hours (like 40+ a week) to studying companies and choosing stocks. Even then, there's nothing saying you're going to be good at it, and plenty of evidence you won't be.

Simple is Better

So what's the answer? I'll let you hear it from Warren Buffett first. When Buffett passes away, he wants his Berkshire Hathaway shares to be distributed to charity. This is what he wants to be done with the remaining cash:

> *"My advice to the trustee couldn't be more simple: Put 10% of the cash in short-term government bonds and 90% in a very low-cost S&P 500 index fund. (I suggest Vanguard's.) I believe the trust's long-term results from this policy will be superior to those attained by most investors — whether pension funds, institutions or individuals — who employ high-fee managers."*
>
> — WARREN BUFFETT

Did you hear that? Index funds.

Most people who devote their time to picking stocks don't beat the market itself. [2] Why buy individual companies when you can buy the market? Or at least most of it. How do you do that? Through index funds. You can thank the late Jack Bogle, founder of Vanguard, for popularizing index funds. He realized the market was beating the vast majority of active mutual fund managers, so he found a way to invest in the market; thus, index funds were created. Thanks, Jack! (Note: Though Jack didn't actually create index funds like many believe, and originally argued against them, he is the one who eventually brought them to the rest of the world.)

It's easy for a beginner investor to start picking stocks and see a few gains. Then they think they must be good at this. I know I thought so. Until I realized my small gains were nowhere close to the massive gains of the market, since we were in an extreme bull market at the time.

It's not just about making big returns. You have to

compare your earnings to the market: the index. The market is the standard. And to consider yourself a good stock picker, you've got to beat it... consistently.

Principles of Investing

Once you know these rules and understand them, you're in the clear. Don't worry, it's easy to grasp.

Here are six rules you can use for successful and easy investing:

1. **Invest in index funds** – I know I sound like a broken record, but the average investor should be investing in index funds. It takes a lot of time to research individual stocks, and spending all that time doesn't guarantee your success. Also, index funds provide automatic diversification within the stock market, which saves your time.
2. **Spend your time elsewhere** – You're better off devoting your time to earning more money, improving yourself, and doing the things you love. Even if you could beat the index by a few points, is it really worth the time you spend? Your time is much more valuable than the *potential* returns.
3. **Avoid paying high fees** – One of the best things about index funds is the low fees. You shouldn't be paying more than 0.5% on a good index fund. And honestly, you shouldn't even be paying that much. I'm with Buffett on Vanguard. I don't usually recommend specific

companies, but they're hard to beat on fees and fund options. No, they didn't pay me to say that.
4. **Avoid taxes as much as possible** – You'll be avoiding high fees with index funds, but you have to watch out for Uncle Sam too. Find the best ways to shelter your money, legally, from taxes. Your company's retirement plan and/or an IRA (Individual Retirement Account) will be your best bet.
5. **Follow Buffet's first rule** – Buffett says the first rule of investing is to not lose money. His second rule reminds you of the first. Why? Because a 50% decline fully offsets a 100% gain. Index funds are well protected. Take more risks when you're young, but don't be stupid.
6. **Time, not timing, is everything** – Don't try to time the market. You can't. I can't. Can George Soros? It's debatable. But we aren't George Soros, and the buy-low-sell-high strategy never happens consistently. Save yourself the time and stress; buy low-cost index funds. Think long-term growth.

If it really is this easy, why don't we hear this information coming from Wall Street? Simple! Because you can't get rich and famous on Wall Street by telling people to passively invest in low-cost index funds, avoid fees, and shelter their money from taxes. There's no sales pitch in that. Jim Cramer would have a short show if he started promoting this idea.

Easy, But Not Easy

This is easy, right? Yes and no. The idea is easy, but the discipline and practice isn't. That's why you set up an automatic investing plan to take discipline out of the equation. Because it's easy to do, but it's just as easy not to do. Not to mention, it seems like a lot more fun to try to pick winning stocks, doesn't it? It's not. Earning a higher return over the long haul will lead to much more fun down the road. But you know that.

That's it. In possibly the shortest section on investing ever, you know the most efficient way to invest for retirement. This isn't the be-all and end-all advice to investing, but it almost is. I know several dividend investors who do well investing in large-cap, individual dividend stocks, but it also takes a lot more time than index investing.

All you really need to take away and remember is this: Invest in low-cost index funds, avoid high fees, and shelter from taxes.

You're not going to hear that on TV.

Summary & Action

Control your money, or your money will control you.

- *Are you taking control of your finances with a budget and/or an automatic spending plan?*

Simple investing is easy and effective.

- *Are you investing in simple index funds with low fees?*

Wealth isn't to make you happy; it's to increase your giving and service.

- *Why do you want wealth?*

Action: Start a budget today. Don't want a budget? Automate everything you can, and live on the rest. Start investing in simple index funds, preferably through a work-related retirement account, or an IRA.

Reflection:

8

SEASONS

Fifteen years ago, if you would've told me I'd be married with five children at this point in my life, I would've laughed at you. Well, that's exactly how life is laughing right now. Life is funny – sometimes it's a "haha" funny; other times, it's an ironic funny.

Seasons—like life in general—are often unexpected and/or unplanned.

I love having a large family, but I do recognize its limitations. For example, I can't go out with my single friends every night if I expect my family to stick around. But I recognize I'm in this season, and being in the season of family, I don't have the desire to leave my family every night and go hang out with friends – I'd rather be with my family.

We're always in a certain season of life – in the middle, or in a transition. And every season is beautiful in its own way, even if it's painful or difficult.

I want to start with a quick parable from an unknown author...

"Four Seasons of a Tree"

There was a man who had four sons. He wanted his sons to learn not to judge things too quickly. So he sent them each on a quest, in turn, to go and look at a pear tree that was a great distance away. The first son went in the winter, the second in the spring, the third in summer, and the youngest son in the fall.

When they had all gone and come back, he called them together to describe what they had seen. The first son said that the tree was ugly, bent, and twisted. The second son said no—it was covered with green buds and full of promise. The third son disagreed; he said it was laden with blossoms that smelled so sweet and looked so beautiful, it was the most graceful thing he had ever seen. The last son disagreed with all of them; he said it was ripe and drooping with fruit, full of life and fulfillment.

The man then explained to his sons that they were all right, because they had each seen but only one season in the tree's life. He told them that you cannot judge a tree, or a person, by only one season, and that the essence of who they are—and the pleasure, joy, and love that come from that life—can only be measured at the end, when all the seasons are complete.

If you give up when it's winter, you will miss the promise of your spring, the beauty of your summer, fulfillment of your fall. Don't let the pain of one season destroy the joy of all the rest. Don't

> *judge life by one difficult season. Persevere throughout the difficult patches and better times are sure to come some time or later.*

This brief story sums up the idea that we're all in one season or another. Plan for your season, and you'll be happier and more productive. If you try to plan as if you're in a season you're not in, you'll never feel fulfilled.

The Seasons of Life

Most people go through the basic seasons: single, married, having children, and eventually, an empty nest. There are also common seasons that prove to be more difficult, such as going through a big move, getting out of serious debt, starting a business, changing careers, fostering, adopting, losing a copious amount of weight, and the list continues...

You also have the challenging seasons. Things like divorce/re-marriage, becoming a widow/widower, dealing with a terminal illness in the family, fighting a legal battle, military deployments, depression, having a special-needs child, or the arduous burden of losing a child.

That seemingly exhaustive list doesn't come close to encompassing all the seasons you could face. Once you start planning and adapting your life to your season, stress and strain will begin to fade. Maybe not entirely, but substantially.

The first step to handling the season you're in is to know and actually recognize which season it is. Once you've accepted that, realize your season has limiting factors.

We don't realize how much time we have when we're single until we get married. Then we don't realize our freedom as a young married couple until we have kids. We don't realize how "easy" one child is until we have two... you get the point.

That's the nature of life. A parent can tell a single person about how much time they have, but we need to actually experience it to fully understand. I'm sure life is like that for a reason, but I haven't figured out the reason yet. As a single person, you may feel like you don't have much free time. You've likely filled your schedule full on your own accord.

I hear it all the time: "I don't know how you guys do everything you do with five kids." My response is always the same: "You'd do it too if you were in my shoes." We—human beings—adapt, overcome, conquer. When we face challenges and difficulties, we either overcome them, or we're overcome by them. It's a choice. Events and circumstances aren't always a choice, but our response is *always* a choice.

Limiting factors are what determine how you live in your season. Once you know and accept your season, it's easy to plan. The more limiting factors, the more planning.

Saying our life is busy and my schedule is full would be an overt understatement. But we handle it with one word: planning. Planning is the difference in making life work for you and life working against you. That's what chapter 6 was all about.

Let's get to the practical application and go over some specific seasons.

The Season of Singleness

When you're single, look at your married friends and friends with kids. Try to realize how much time you do have. Right now, it's all about you (planning-wise). You may not feel like it, but it is.

This is the perfect season to:

- Write a book
- Build a successful career
- Find your ideal partner for marriage
- Start a business or a side hustle and go all in
- Spend time with friends and build relationships
- Devote yourself to a cause bigger than yourself (e.g., missionary work, Peace Corps, military, etc.)
- Ultimately, work on yourself. Grow. Learn. Prepare.

You have the time to do something big right now – something that takes a lot of time. Use all of the time you have while you have it. Prepare and plan for when you don't have this much time.

The Season of Marriage

Once you get married, it's not all about you anymore. But

you've still got a lot of time. You may be looking for a home, and making big life decisions. Things like career choices, location choices, and whether or not to have kids now, later, or at all. You have a lot of decisions to make with your spouse.

This is the perfect season to:

- Figure out where you want to live your life
- Get your house in order and make career decisions
- Attend marriage seminars to strengthen your bond
- Get to know your spouse and develop a deep relationship
- Have an active social life and develop relationships with other couples
- Start a side hustle that doesn't compete with your spouse for attention

You have time. Use it wisely and prepare. A child is coming. A wise person once said, "First comes love, then comes marriage, then comes the baby in the baby carriage."

The Season of Children

Having children is likely the biggest change you've experienced so far. Don't worry. You'll go through periods where you feel like you have no time—especially in the beginning—but these times are temporary. You will start to get your time back soon.

It is kind of weird to go from living alone to living with your spouse, but you've been living with other people your whole life. It's unlikely you've been taking care of children your whole life (I know some big brothers and sisters are disagreeing right now).

Hopefully, you've prepared for this season financially and physically, but even if you aren't prepared, you've got this. Thousands of children are brought into this world every day to parents who aren't prepared. Honestly, it's impossible to fully prepare for your first child, but any advance planning you do will help enormously.

You may feel like your life is over and your free time is gone, but that's not the case at all. Your priorities have changed. That's all.

This is the perfect season to:

- Focus on your family, spend time together and get your house in order
- Start a side hustle that doesn't interfere with family time (e.g., early mornings or late nights)
- Work to provide for your family, but it's not the season to work 100 hours a week — speaking from experience

You should be focusing on your family right now. Especially in the early years. I constantly had people telling me I was working too much when I first started my family, but I kept saying, "I'll cut back once I [insert whatever the next life event was at the time]," or, "I'm just working this much now, but I won't continue like this forever." I didn't continue like that forever (because I finally learned my lesson), but I missed a lot of my first daughter's early years due to my work, and I can't get that time back.

I wish I would've listened and cut back then, instead of years later. Take it from someone who has been there: don't use these years to make all the money you can, use them to be with your family. You don't need as much money as you think you do.

The Season of Adoption

Adoption has been one of the most rewarding things we've ever done. But as far as seasons, it's really just about taking the time to allow the adopted children to adapt. Take some time off work. Take a vacation if possible. Allow time for bonding. Make their first memories in your home sweet ones. Don't rush the process. Depending on their age(s), it will take more, less, or no time for them to adapt, but you should allow for that time.

The Season of an Empty Nest

We are far from this stage, but it's coming. By the time you reach this stage, you probably have a good idea as to what you want to do with the rest of your life. You could be writing this book. By this point in life, my wife and I should be down to only ministry and travel – we know plans almost always change.

This is the perfect season to:

- Travel the country or the world
- Get your house like you want it, or build a new one (finances permitting)

- Write that book, create that product, or whatever else you've been putting off
- Do the things you've wanted to do, but haven't found time for

This is the stage where you can appreciate the amount of time you have, above all other stages. You should be able to do anything you want!

Special Seasons

For the sake of time and space, when I say "special seasons," I'm referring to every season other than what I just mentioned. The main thing the other seasons have in common is this: something fairly rare and/or unexpected comes into your life, and you must make it your priority, whether you want to or not. Most of the time, you should be focusing on *getting through* this season, and not much outside of that.

Whether it's moving out of your town, divorce, remarriage, grieving a loss, a military deployment, or awaiting legal results, you will have to put most of your attention towards this season. Focus on getting through... sometimes as quickly as you can.

That being said, in every season, *appreciate the days*. Don't get so caught up on counting the days until something is over that you waste those days, months, or years. Regardless of our situation, we can rejoice in the Lord and be joyful, just as Paul did in the New Testament when he was in prison.

I don't want to speak on seasons I don't have much experience in, but I do want to briefly touch on them, because there's a good chance you're going through one of these difficult seasons right now...

Seasons That Change Your Life

These are some difficult seasons:

- A special needs child
- Terminal illness
- Losing a child

What do these have in common? They all alter the rest of your life, and they're unexpected. Whether the terminal illness applies to you, your spouse, or a child, it will affect you in one way or another.

SPECIAL NEEDS CHILD

My wife has a heart for people, and especially children, with special needs. With God working how He does in our life, it wouldn't surprise me if He entrusted a special-needs child to us. But for now, we haven't had direct experience with this.

The most important part of caring for another person who requires a lot of attention, whether a special-needs child or an ill parent, is seeing the experience as day-to-day. People who have personally dealt with this—I know several people who have—say you can't look at it from a lifelong perspective. Don't ask, "can I really take care of this person for the rest of their life?" Ask, "can I take care of this person today?" I guarantee the answer will always be yes.

Day-to-day thinking will help you appreciate your time with them and keep you from getting overwhelmed. Reach out to your support network. Family and friends often come through in large numbers for people who face times such as these. If you don't have a strong enough support network, reach out to some different organizations or groups online who are going through the same thing.

Terminal Illness

I'm referencing any terminal illness under your roof. It could be you, your spouse, an extended family member, a child. You should give the person—even if it's you—the fullest life imaginable. The Make-A-Wish Foundation specializes in this, but you can do it yourself. Let them live out their final years by doing everything they've always wanted to and dreamed of doing. It's not about how long you live, but about how you live while you're here. Help them work on their relationship with Jesus. Help them appreciate life.

Losing a Child

I couldn't imagine going through this, and if you have, let me just say, I give you my most sincere condolences. You're an extremely strong person emotionally, and even though you may not feel like it now, this experience will probably be your largest season of growth.

If this were to happen to me, I would pray my heart out. I would lean on God to get me through each day and lead me into recovery, even if I never fully felt recovered (I've been told you never really do). Some great friends of ours recently lost their child when he was a young adult – their strength in trusting God through it all has been inspiring. If nothing else, knowing you will be with them again will get you through.

While I don't believe everything happens for a reason (because that would mean the most grotesque pieces of history happened for a reason), I do believe God can always bring good even out of the worst situations. We live in a fallen world with principalities and powers of evil at work. Much is the work of Satan, and some is the product of a fallen world, but God has a way of turning grim to good.

The important thing to know in situations like this is that it's ok to be sad. I'm not a psychiatrist or a medical doctor, and I'm not giving professional advice, but you shouldn't need anti-depressants if you just lost a child, you should be sad. You have every right to be sad. Sadness, crying, and mourning are the natural ways to begin healing. I know anti-depressants have their place—I'm not against them—but let yourself grieve properly. Turning to medication immediately can hinder the natural process of grieving.

Season-Tailored Advice

The most important takeaway from all of this is to tailor any advice to your season. Take podcasts, for example. It seems like some of the most popular podcasts are delivered by fairly young, single guys and gals. You shouldn't expect to implement everything they're doing if you're no longer in the single season (maybe find a different podcast).

That also shouldn't be an excuse. You can always do more than you think you can do, but don't try to do more than you know you should do. So take the advice, consider the season you're in, and decide the best way to implement said advice. I haven't been through every season, but I've been through many. I can't tell you what to do in each season, but you can figure it out on your own, if you recognize where you are, and work with what you've got.

Summary & Action

We're all in a different season.

- *Which season are you in?*

We can't control the season we're in, but we can control how we respond to it.

- *How are you responding to the season you're in?*

You may have more time than you think in your season.

- *What's something more you could be doing in your season?*

Action: Use the season you're in. Make the most of it.

As far as other people are concerned, you never know what season they're in. It could be a season of depression, masked by a seemingly happy life, whether single, married, or married with children. We only know what we see, and that's typically around 1% of what someone is actually going through. Just be kind. It's that simple.

Reflection:

9

SELF

Do you know what is one of the most important things you can grasp about your productivity? Self-awareness.

And because of that, I want you to really take it in. Don't just blow this off and act like you already knew it, even if you did know its importance. Hear me out.

The One Thing

I'm going to say it again, because it's that important. The one thing that can have more impact on your productivity than anything else is self-awareness. I've mentioned before how important energy is to your productivity. Without energy, you're not going to do much. Of course, self-discipline is equally important. And yes, you need to be creating positive habits and planning your days. But self-awareness will be the biggest factor in staying productive, increasing your productivity, and ultimately, maximizing it.

Self-awareness is simply the process of watching personal trends, analyzing your performance, and being honest.

Here's a great example of how a lack of self-awareness can defeat you...

A Story About Forced Mornings

John had always been a night owl, but one day he decided to make a change. John was going to become a morning person. He'd always heard mornings are the most productive time of the day, and he's been told you can accomplish more before 8:00am than most people accomplish in a week.

So he tried it...

It was difficult for John to wake up at first, but after a few weeks, he began to wake up much earlier than he was used to. And he found the morning to be a great time to be productive. About a month later, John went on vacation. While on vacation, John slept in every day and woke up without an alarm clock, which meant waking up much later.

After his vacation, he found it difficult to return to his early morning routine, but he was certain he could get back into it. For several weeks, John would set his alarm clock for 5:00am (the time he was waking up before vacation). However, now John found himself hitting the snooze until it was time for him to get ready for work (around 8:00am). He was growing more and more frustrated, because he would put things off until morning, expecting to wake up early, but then he would constantly be defeated by the dreaded snooze button.

After several months of not waking up as scheduled, John finally decided to try using nights instead of early mornings. A few weeks into this new idea, he discovered he was able to accomplish more at night than he ever could in the morning. Even when he was getting up early, he had a difficult time concentrating, but he's now getting more done than ever… at night.

So what's the lesson here? John is a night owl. His mind just works better at night. Many people find that they are more creative and more productive at night, despite the fact that many productivity books, blogs, and articles promote mornings as the best time to get things done. For me, and many others, mornings really are the best. For John, he preferred nights.

The point is, don't fool yourself.

Are You Self-Aware?

Obviously, this isn't about being a morning person or a night owl, it's about self-awareness and self-honesty. You must be honest with yourself to reach your full potential. It's easy to fall into the trap of trying to create a hundred new positive habits in one week.

If you don't currently work out, you're setting yourself up for failure by starting with a one-hour, intense workout every day. If you don't have a current reading habit, your setting yourself up for failure by committing to reading a book a week, right out of the gate. I developed a checklist to determine which time of day is best for you, and when you can get the most done. Use it to mold your life, and then start molding all of the productivity advice you intake to your new, self-aware self.

Self-Awareness Checklist

Here are some specific questions to determine your level of self-awareness, and maximize your productivity.

Proceed with caution, these questions may force you to be honest with yourself, and that can be scary:

- Are you a morning person or a night person? Be honest.
- Do you keep your word with yourself? Do you actually do what you say you'll do?
- Is there a difference between your exercise "schedule" and the times you actually exercise?
- Do you actually read as much as you like to think you read?
- When do you have the most energy? After exercise? After sleep? When you're hungry/full?
- Do you spend more time learning about productivity than you spend taking action?
- Do you actually have written goals? Seriously? No, seriously.

All of these questions will help you take a survey of what works and doesn't work in your life. Hopefully, these questions will make you think. Take the time to sit down and answer each one of these — elaborate, even on the yes-no questions. Increase your self-awareness and you'll learn where to focus your time and energy. You'll learn a lot about yourself just by answering these questions.

When dealing with yourself, the biggest factors that can get you off course faster than anything are worry and stress. Both can lead to depression, and both will ensure you live an unhappy life. Let's talk about worry, and we'll get into stress.

Dealing With Worry

When I uprooted my family, moved from the US to Italy, and dealt with several serious family concerns along the way (including the death of my last living grandparent), I dealt with some worry. It was rough, and while I had never considered myself a worrier, I worried myself sick a few times over several months.

Throughout the move, we didn't have a home of our own for two months. Two months might not seem like that long, but being temporarily homeless is tough on a father. Even though we were actively looking for a place to live, I know my children felt uncomfortable, especially since we were sharing a hotel room the entire time. They wanted a home. They wanted *their* home.

I tried to tell myself, "some children never have a home; at least I'm trying." Trying to play the "so many people have it harder than I do" card, but when you're living in the moment, you handle it based on your current circumstances. That's why people who are literally starving can often handle it better than someone who is simply unhappy with their job. We can handle more than we think, and how much we can handle depends a lot on how much we've handled in the past. There's that adversity again.

Well, my wife and kids got their home eventually. We

found a beautiful home, and my stress subsided. The worry, for the most part, was over. My job was still quite stressful (I am a War Planner, after-all), and we weren't completely settled, but I grew as a person more in those months than I did over the five years before.

Worry is one of the leading causes of death, though it's usually disguised in some form of physical disease or sickness. But worry is at the root of so many issues patients are dealing with in hospitals all over the world. I have learned techniques to handle worry that actually work, and I still use them today. I know there will be plenty of trying times in the future. That's why it's important to learn how to deal with worry and stress now.

Many of these techniques are adapted from Dale Carnegie's book, *How to Stop Worrying and Start Living*, because it was like a second bible to me during my most worrisome times. If you deal with worry on any level, you need to read that book.

So how do you handle worry? Here's how...

1. The "Two Week" Attitude

One way to deal with worry is to ask yourself a question:

"Will I be worried about this in two weeks?"

If the answer is no, then what's the point of worrying about it right now? Think about all the things you were worried about last week, month, and year. Sure, some things stick with us, some things are more serious than others, but overall, worry is so often temporary.

Worry itself is never helpful. It's good to be

concerned, and a small amount of stress can actually help motivate us, but *worry* is never a good thing.

2. What's the Worst That Could Happen?

I don't mean these to be famous last words. This isn't a "hold my beer and watch this" type of question.

When you're dealing with a situation, ask yourself seriously, "what's the worst that could happen?"

And even if the worst is really bad, you must accept that as a possible outcome. Once you've accepted the worst possible outcome, you can accept anything that happens. You'll be surprised how the worry disappears.

What if the worst is losing your job, or even worse, losing a loved one? You have to deal with that outcome. If that happened, you would keep moving forward. You can always find another job. In time, you will be able to deal with the loss of a loved one. No matter the outcome, if you accept the worst now, you have nothing to worry about. And, besides...

3. It Probably Won't Happen

> *"I've had a lot of worries in my life, most of which never happened."*
>
> — Mark Twain

Around 85% of what we worry about never happens. [1] If we remember there is a good chance what we're worrying about won't actually happen, we can calm down. It doesn't always work, but it helps.

We are worrisome creatures. Sometimes this actually takes verbally telling yourself to calm down and stop worrying. I've fought with myself before over worries and thoughts that don't deserve space in my mind.

Why worry when you can stay positive or pray about the issue?

> *"Do not be anxious about anything, but in everything by prayer and supplication with thanksgiving let your requests be made known to God."*
>
> — PHILIPPIANS 4:6

4. DAY-TIGHT COMPARTMENTS

In, *How to Stop Worrying and Start Living*, Dale talks about "day-tight compartments." A ship has water-tight compartments that can fill with water, be shut off from the rest of the ship, and keep the ship afloat. This is how we must view our days: one day at a time. Worry about today if you must, but don't worry about tomorrow.

> *"Therefore do not be anxious about tomorrow, for tomorrow will be anxious for itself. Sufficient for the day is its own trouble."*
>
> — MATTHEW 6:34

5. DO SOMETHING RADICAL

If you're dealing with an immense issue that's worrying you to death, there's a final option that works in some circumstances. The idea is to make a huge change. This might seem counterproductive, but it often isn't. You may be dealing with a lot right now, and you may need to get away.

Here are a few options depending on the situation:

- **Take an extended vacation** – This doesn't have to be expensive. You could go on a long hike or camping trip, and spend next to nothing.
- **Move to a different state/country** – Doing this caused worry for me due to the circumstances, but if your worry is all tied to where you live, try making a radical change by moving far away.
- **Quit your job** – Your job may be the main stress-factor in your life. Why do you still work there? Life is short and there are always other jobs out there. Don't let your job kill you.

Sometimes the radical choice is the right choice. Don't do anything radical without first counting the costs, but life is too short to be stuck in a situation that is detrimental to your health. It comes down to this: if a situation can be changed, change it. If it can't be changed, don't worry about it. Even if the outcome could be severe, worrying won't help.

Worrying will never make things better. It will always make things worse. However, we all know it's difficult to simply stop worrying. That's where some more practices come in that can help. Enter: meditation.

Meditation

Meditation and prayer, and the combination of the two, have helped more people than we will ever know, and when you're dealing with worry (or life in general), mediation can be your answer to get through. Meditation has been around for centuries, and yet, it can still be a controversial topic.

Most of the people who recommend meditating start by saying something like, "I know you think this is some sort of eastern ritual," or, "you might think you have to be Buddhist to meditate". I admit, it does carry that connotation, or at least it used to. I'll spare you. I'm going to assume you're wanting to implement meditation as a self-improvement tactic, or as a way to clear your mind and increase your focus.

That being said, here's a guide to meditation for the average person who wants more clarity and a clear mind...

Benefits of Meditation

This is a simple starting place. Let's talk about the benefits of meditation. Then we'll get into the "how."

Meditation makes you more productive in several ways. It also makes your life better in general, and this is how:

- Meditation increases mental strength [2]

- Meditation increases brain activity [3]
- Meditation increases your focus
- Meditation gives you energy
- Meditation calms your mind [4]
- Meditation decreases anxiety
- Meditation improves your mood
- Meditation increases your creativity
- Meditation increases overall happiness

Are you ready to meditate yet? Research has even shown meditation boosts students' test scores, and even helped people to perform better on less sleep. Sure, you need to get an adequate amount of sleep, but meditation will help you after those short nights.

Here's how to actually do it...

How to Start Meditating

You may be a strong thinker, but you'd be surprised at how much of your life just happens... passively. Meditation will improve your level of thinking, and it will also help you rest your mind. There's a middle ground between overthinking and passively living.

To start meditating, first, realize it's easier than it sounds. You must realize this, because when you first start doing it, it will feel "too easy," and that's how it should feel. You simply start by sitting in a comfortable position, and then you focus on your breathing. When your mind wanders and other thoughts begin to pop into your head, bring your mind back to your breath. By doing this, you're training your mind. This is the beginning of meditation, and it only gets better from here.

Here are some tips to make it more effective:

- **Start small** – Even if you only have five minutes—or even two—to meditate each day, start with that. The smaller you start, the easier it will be, which means you'll be more likely to stick with it.
- **Find quiet** – It's hard to sit in a comfortable position, and focus on your breath, if there's a lot of background noise. Find a time during the day when you can sit in complete silence. Or use earplugs.
- **Be still** – If you're a fidgety person, and have a hard time being still (I'm a drummer, so I understand), make it a priority to be still. It may take practice, but you'll eventually stop moving while you meditate.
- **Use mornings** – While evenings before bed are a great time for meditation, I've found that meditating in the mornings is best to get your day off to a good start. Or why not just do both?
- **Start now** – You may think you're not ready to begin, but it's so simple, just start now. You may be terrible at focusing on your breath at first, but that's why you keep doing it, over and over.
- **Smile** – This is personal preference, but I find that smiling helps when you first start. Once you're truly focused, you'll probably forget whether you're smiling or not, but it creates a positive start.

- **Try guided** – If you're having difficulty focusing or you don't like the idea of sitting alone and only focusing on your breath, try a guided meditation. They are helpful for the beginners and the experienced.

I hope you enjoy meditation from the beginning, but many times it can seem difficult and almost frustrating for beginners. It's easy to *try* to meditate, but it's harder to actually do it effectively. At first, you'll muddle your way through a few minutes with one eye on the clock. After a while, you'll need to set an alarm, because you'll get lost in meditation. That's a good place to be.

Remember, this is one method of meditating. Focusing on your breath may be the most popular method for westerners today, but there are hundreds of different ways to meditate. You may find meditation to be a great time for prayer. It's great for that too. This is just the beginning.

There's a bright future full of focus and clarity ahead.

Summary & Action

Self-awareness is the key to a productive life.

- *Are you aware of how you work, and what works best for you?*

Worry and stress can ruin you.

- *How do you respond to worry and stress in your daily life?*

It's important to care for others, but we can't forget about ourselves.

- *Are you taking time for yourself to grow, learn, and relax?*

Action: Become more self-aware. Figure out what works for you. Track your daily habits and rituals to figure out where you can make improvements.

Reflection:

10

GOD

God is the most important part of every decision I make. I wrote this chapter because the audience of this book is high achievers, entrepreneurs, and people who want more out of life. If you're growing, learning, and trying to get better, you're likely in this category, and that's why you're reading this book.

The thing is, I noticed a trend among people with this "elite" mindset, who are constantly trying to get better: they're often sad, depressed, and lonely, despite the seemingly successful lifestyle they may live. Why is that? I have a few guesses, but my first would be God not being part of their lives.

When you think big, you have to believe in something bigger than yourself. Too often, people fully give themselves to earthy things like money, careers, businesses, success, or something else that's never going to make them truly happy. You'll never find happiness by chasing it.

> *"I wish everyone could get rich and famous and everything they ever dreamed of so they can see that's not the answer."*
>
> — JIM CARREY

No amount of earthly success is going to make you happy. Without God, there will always be a void. I'm going to get into what success looks like, through the lens of Jesus, but first, let's talk about the different views of God around the world.

World Religions

I've met people from many different religions… Muslim, Jewish, Catholic, Orthodox, Hindu, Buddhist, Satanist, and everything in between. In my experience, people actually want to have a decent conversation.

In general, our world strays away from topics like religion because people often don't know what they believe, and we are typically non-confrontational when it comes to these points. Americans stray away from "religion and politics" more than any other people-group I've met. I've had great experiences by leading freely into these conversations on sensitive topics, and as long as I'm not a jerk, these are some of the most edifying conversations I've ever had.

I love discussing religion. I'm mostly interested in finding out what people believe and why. That's the best place to start for me to explain my beliefs and apologetics, and to hear theirs. When you look at the world religions, most people in the US claim to be Christian, whether Protestant, Catholic, Orthodox, or simply a Jesus Follower – my personal favorite label, if I had to choose one. The other religions carry a small percentage of the country. When you examine each one individually, it's easy to see how they all relate in many ways. For example, the Quran mentions Jesus often... more than it mentions their primary prophet, Muhammad. And there are accounts of a global flood as well as creation stories throughout almost every religion.

I've heard the Universalism viewpoint stressed quite a bit – the belief that all religions lead to one god, and that any path works to get to heaven. The problem is, that doesn't line up with any one of the religions' holy books. The Bible has one of the most explicit examples of this exclusivity:

> *Jesus said to him, "I am the way, and the truth, and the life. No one comes to the Father except through me. If you had known me, you would have known my Father also. From now on you do know him and have seen him."*
>
> *Philip said to him, "Lord, show us the Father, and it is enough for us." Jesus said to him, "Have I been with you so long, and you still do not know me, Philip? Whoever has seen me has seen the Father. How can you say, 'Show us the Father'? Do you not believe that I am in the Father and the Father is in me? The words that I say to you I do not speak on my own authority, but the Father who dwells in me does his works. Believe me that I am*

> *in the Father and the Father is in me, or else
> believe on account of the works themselves.*
>
> — JOHN 14:6-11

I know you've probably heard this verse many times before now, but that's because of its exclusivity. It's offensive. But you simply cannot believe these verses, and believe that all people will enter heaven, through whichever route they choose. It's hard to swallow, but that doesn't make it untrue.

There's a difference between God and religion. God is great. Religion is poison. God calls us to come to Him, through Jesus. Religion causes people to do insane things, like the Crusades, mass murder, manipulation, and events such as the People's Temple leading and forcing people to literally "drink the Kool-Aid," resulting in the single greatest loss of American civilian life in a deliberate act, prior to 9/11.

Religion has been one of the leading causes of murder and death throughout history. When I say religion here, I'm referring to the act of humans trying to reach a god, and/or following rules set by a god. Following Jesus is about God sending His Son to us, not us trying to reach Him. That's the difference between Christianity and other world religions.

I love Jesus and my relationship with Him, but when it turns into following religious rules, I'm out. I follow the Bible, and try my best to live a life like Jesus, because of who He is, not because of some religious set of rules. I understand my salvation comes through faith, not works (Ephesians 2:8-9). Even as Christians, our righteousness comes through Christ, not the law (Galatians 2:21, Romans 8:3). I also understand faith without works is dead, but the works have to come out of the faith, not the reverse (James 2:14-26).

I'm ok with lumping historical Christianity, which I refer to as Christendom, into "poisonous religion." I get that my view isn't popular and that many Christians defend the historical church, but I simply can't. It was, however, religion, not Jesus, that ultimately led to the dreadful church history we have today, and the Christian Church history is dreadful.

We should lead Godly lives to our best ability. We should strive to walk in the will of Christ every step of the way. But we do need to do away with the religious and self-righteous attitude of simply following rules and earning our way into heaven. Jesus didn't come to rebuke the blatant sinners as much as He came to rebuke the religious.

Religion, including evolutionary beliefs, has led people to do horrific things. People do these things because they have a certain belief. It may be that they feel like God told them to kill 50 people, or it could be that since we all just evolved from animals, killing others is no different from a lion killing a gazelle. And with no god, and no objective morality, no one can argue that killing (in that sense) is wrong, because morality would be left up to individuals to determine.

The underlying point is, while there are religions with books that encourage murder, Jesus never did. Jesus encouraged peace, even to the point of loving your enemies – no matter what! You don't see that in other "religious leaders."

People can be terrible, and people have done many atrocities in the name of religion. Just as many, if not more people, have done horrible things due to the lack of any belief in a god. Because that eventually leads to a belief that people are technically just animals.

I follow Jesus, and I don't believe anything He said could lead someone to violent acts. Say what you will about the Hebrew Bible—the Old Testament—but Jesus and the New Testament are Christ revealed, while the Old Testament is Christ concealed. Anything in the Old Testament must be viewed through the lens of Jesus, not the other way around. And Jesus is pure love.

While religion may be poisonous, there's nothing poisonous about Jesus. Jesus calls us to live loving, productive lives, and that's what we're going to talk about in this chapter...

A Fruitful Christian Life

We all want to be productive. We want to live a fruitful life. Productive employees, spouses, parents... productive people. But how is productivity different for Christians? There is the worldly view of productivity and success – producing more, purely to earn more money and more worldly success.

The worldly view of productivity encompasses your business life and parts of your personal life. In a way, productivity for a Christian is backward, because the secondary parts of worldly productivity are often first for Christians.

This isn't just about earning more money, though that's not a bad thing. This isn't just about getting more work done, though that's part of it. This is about living a productive Christian life — a *fruitful* life.

Let's start with the main way Christian productivity differs from worldly productivity...

Jesus is First

To be a productive Christian, we must actively pursue a relationship with Jesus first, putting our family second, and our ministry next. Don't get caught in the trap of equating church to God, and putting your ministry before your family. Some people put their ministry before God, making their ministry an idol. If anything misses Jesus' entire point, it's that.

Nothing in your life is productive if you don't have a relationship with Jesus first. Remember how I said Christian productivity is backward from worldly productivity? Prayer, reading your Bible, and meditating on God's Word are the building blocks of Christian productivity – those areas determine everything else.

Business productivity is part of the equation. We all want to build companies and organizations that help people, and, ultimately, spread Christ to the world. But if you don't focus on your relationship with Jesus first, the rest is not going to come willingly.

Time management, self-development, and success teaching are often criticized by Christians, because a lot of it is about greed and selfishness. When practicing productivity, as with anything, it's a matter of the heart. When we're devouring productivity books, reading blogs, and always finding ways to become more productive, we have to make sure we keep our focus in the right place.

It's not about you getting the most you can out of life, it's about giving the most you can with your life.

So the order of things is:

- Make sure God comes first
- Make sure your heart is right
- Be as productive as you choose

Make your ultimate goal pleasing and serving God. When your ultimate goal becomes getting things done, being more productive, making more money, and pleasing yourself, you're crossing over into a worldly view.

Productivity can turn into an idol if you let it.

When we accomplish goals and complete simple tasks, endorphins are released in our brains, which gives a sense of satisfaction. We can actually become addicted to that endorphin rush, which may be God's natural way of motivating us, but if we start to idolize the "high" we get when we're productive, we need to reevaluate our priorities.

The Bible on Productivity

There's plenty in the Bible about living productively, for the Father. Jesus teaches a lot on how we should live. It's obvious that He is about taking action, not just living day-to-day, and going through the motions. Here's what Jesus says about the *branches* that lead to a *fruitful* life:

> *"I am the true vine, and my Father is the vinedresser. Every branch in me that does not bear fruit he*

takes away, and every branch that does bear fruit he prunes, that it may bear more fruit. Already you are clean because of the word that I have spoken to you. Abide in me, and I in you. As the branch cannot bear fruit by itself, unless it abides in the vine, neither can you, unless you abide in me. I am the vine; you are the branches. Whoever abides in me and I in him, he it is that bears much fruit, for apart from me you can do nothing. If anyone does not abide in me he is thrown away like a branch and withers; and the branches are gathered, thrown into the fire, and burned. If you abide in me, and my words abide in you, ask whatever you wish, and it will be done for you. By this my Father is glorified, that you bear much fruit and so prove to be my disciples. As the Father has loved me, so have I loved you. Abide in my love. If you keep my commandments, you will abide in my love, just as I have kept my Father's commandments and abide in his love. These things I have spoken to you, that my joy may be in you, and that your joy may be full."

— JOHN 15:1-11

Jesus talked a lot, throughout the Gospels, about producing fruit. Obviously, there is no greater wisdom than God himself, so when Jesus told a parable, it was for a specific purpose. But Jesus wasn't the only one to talk about productivity. Proverbs has countless helpful verses...

Productivity Proverbs

THE VALUE OF HARD WORK AND DILIGENCE:

Whoever works his land will have plenty of bread, but he who follows worthless pursuits lacks sense. (Proverbs 12:11)
The hand of the diligent will rule, while the slothful will be put to forced labor. (Proverbs 12:24)
The way of a sluggard is like a hedge of thorns, but the path of the upright is a level highway. (Proverbs 15:19)

ACTION SPEAKS LOUDER THAN WORDS:

In all toil there is profit, but mere talk tends only to poverty. (Proverbs 14:23)

THE IMPORTANCE OF PLANNING:

Without counsel plans fail, but with many advisers they succeed. (Proverbs 15:22)
Commit your work to the LORD, and your plans will be established. (Proverbs 16:3)
The plans of the heart belong to man, but the answer of the tongue is from the LORD. (Proverbs 16:1)
Many are the plans in the mind of a man, but it is the purpose of the LORD that will stand. (Proverbs 19:21)
The plans of the diligent lead surely to abundance, but everyone who is hasty comes only to poverty. (Proverbs 21:5)

Biblically, productivity means living for Jesus, bringing people to salvation, helping others, feeding people, listening to people's struggles... ultimately, it means being Jesus to others, because for some, you may be the closest they ever come to seeing Jesus.

Become a Fruitful Christian

I don't like to broadly discuss things like productivity and living a fruitful life without giving some practical and actionable steps to take. So here are 10 things we can do to become more fruitful Christians:

1. **Track your time** – Know where your time is going and be mindful of how you spend it. You don't have to track your time every day for the rest of your life, but you should at least track it for a month to figure out if your time and your priorities match up.
2. **Plan your days** – Before you go to sleep each night, plan the next day. Plan time for everything on this list, and plan time for the most important priorities in your life. If it's important, it goes into your plan.
3. **Stay organized** – Organize your day, organize your finances, organize your time. Staying organized helps you keep your mind on the things that really matter. Organizing also helps reduce stress, which promotes your focus on God.
4. **Start in prayer** – Begin each day in God's Word, reading the Scripture and praying. Meditate on God's Word. Renew your mind each morning before you go out into the world. Wake up early and discipline yourself

to spend your first waking hours with God
(Proverbs 20:13). Ask God for spiritual peace.
Ask God to show you His Will throughout the
day. Start small by spending five minutes each
morning praying and asking for guidance.
5. **Take care of yourself** – God not only blessed
you with the gift of life, but He also gave you a
body to live it in. Take care of it. Get enough
rest, exercise regularly, and eat healthful meals.
You reap what you sow, so you will be blessed
in the areas you take care of (Galatians 6:7).
6. **Worship joyfully** – Worship shouldn't just
happen on Sunday mornings. Worship should
be a minute-to-minute practice – a way of
living. Devote yourself to joyful worship, in
spirit and in truth (John 4:24).
7. **Walk in integrity** – Be consistent. Do what
you say. Say what you mean and mean what
you say (Proverbs 14:23). Your family and
friends should be able to rely on you to keep
your word.
8. **Listen to the Holy Spirit** – God sent the Holy
Spirit as a Helper, so we know how to live and
what God is calling us to do (John 14:26). Listen
to the still, small voice of the Holy Spirit.
Nothing could be more fruitful.
9. **Focus on today** – Set long-term goals and
think about the future, but take it one day at a
time. It's important to not get ahead of
yourself, and to maximize your hours today,
instead of living in the future or the past, and

the "what-ifs" that each one holds (Proverbs 27:1).
10. **Think long-term** – These last two points are not opposites; they should be used in conjunction with one another. Yes, you must focus on today, since that's all you can control, but you need to have a clear, defined plan for the rest of your life.

Devote each day to God, pray for guidance, and you will live a fruitful life. You will be successful, but what does success look like in the Christian life?

Christian Success

What does success mean to you? Society measures success by money. When someone is "successful," it often means they're financially or professionally successful. For example, Success Magazine is completely devoted to financial and business success, and that's the world's entire view of success.

But what does that really have to do with success?

According to the Bible, financial or business success is a tiny part of success. Webster defines success as simply, "a favorable or desired outcome," granted it also goes on to include the attainment of wealth in the definition, but I think it's evolved into that based on society's view of success.

The question isn't, "what does success mean to the world?", the question is, "what does success mean to you?"

So... what does it mean? Is it important? How important?

Does Success Matter?

> *"Try not to become a man of success but rather try to become a man of value."*
>
> — Albert Einstein

From a Biblical perspective, attaining wealth isn't the ultimate goal, though it's also not a bad thing. Many of the greatest people in the Old Testament had great wealth. But how should Christians really measure success? We may consider one Christian more successful than the other if he seems to be better at keeping the commandments of God. I know we would never admit to that, but we do it – subconsciously.

I'm guilty of measuring myself up to other Christians.

"How did I perform today?"

"At least I don't sin as much as that guy!"

These are things that go through my head, and hopefully I take hold of these thoughts, nail them to the Cross, and find better things to muse on, but often I don't. Often, I don't realize I'm measuring my success in this way until I've been doing it for a while. I have, however, found a way to gauge success as a Christian that seems to be both Biblical and effective. It serves as a great reminder.

Measuring Success

When I think of success, I try to keep one thing in mind:

There is nothing I can do—no way I can perform—that will make God love me any more or less than He does right now, at this very moment. I cannot contribute to my salvation since it has nothing to do with me and everything to do with Christ.

That being said, we can measure our success by asking a few questions:

- Am I growing in my understanding that Christ did everything for me, and I can't do anything to save myself?
- Is my character growing every day in a way that aligns with God's Word and His plan for my life?
- Am I acting in a Christ-like way towards others (e.g., feeding the hungry, serving the poor, etc.)?

For I was hungry and you gave me food, I was thirsty and you gave me drink, I was a stranger and you welcomed me, I was naked and you clothed me, I was sick and you visited me, I was in prison and you came to me.'

— MATTHEW. 25:35

As Albert Einstein said, it's better to measure our value than our success. Value and character go a long way. And both are more important than the typical worldly view of success. In fact, even the unbelievers will tell you character is a requirement for true success, which is part of the reason I wrote an entire chapter on it. True success and happiness can only stem from good character. That being said, what about all of the business and financial success? Is it wrong to strive for that?

Success and the Bible

Christianity isn't about living "your best life now," or building up material possessions to "show people what God did for you." However, God wants to bless us, and this type of success often comes with having a full and fruitful life. I'm investing for retirement. I have money saved. I like to buy nice things, and I'm sure you do too. The key point here isn't to make this type of success your primary focus in life. I've read too many books and articles about how diligent and focused you have to be on your number one goal to be a success.

I'm sure if I developed a product, and focused on nothing else for five or ten years, I could make millions and live in a mansion. You could too. And often, as Christians who want to grow and become better versions of ourselves, we want to set goals and crush them. That's great. We should. But we have to keep Jesus at the center, or it's all going to be in vain.

Proverbs gives us a great starting place:

Commit your work to the Lord, and your plans will be established.

— PROVERBS 16:3

The Psalms tell us God will give us our heart's desires if we delight in Him (Psalm 37:4). This is great news, because it means we don't have to worry about all of these things. We only have to worry about focusing on God. He will trust us with the amount of riches, prosperity, and success we can handle...

One who is faithful in a very little is also faithful in much, and one who is dishonest in a very little is also dishonest in much. If then you have not been faithful in the unrighteous wealth, who will entrust to you the true riches?

— LUKE 16:10-11

All will work itself out for good when we trust in Him (Romans 8:28). Don't worry about not being successful enough, or starting late in the game, or having fewer dollar signs than you would like on the end of your retirement account. Rejoice in the Lord...

Rejoice in the Lord always; again I will say, rejoice. Let your reasonableness be known to everyone. The Lord is at hand; do not be anxious about anything, but in everything by prayer and supplication with thanksgiving let your requests be made known to God. And the peace of God, which surpasses all

> *understanding, will guard your hearts and your minds in Christ Jesus.*
>
> — Philippians 4:4-7

Don't worry or be anxious about these things. I say this, because I know I have a tendency to worry about things like, "Am I going to get that job, promotion, raise, etc.?". If you stay focused on God, His Will is going to be done in your life.

It really comes down to seeking the Kingdom of God first:

> *Therefore, do not be anxious, saying, 'What shall we eat?' or 'What shall we drink?' or 'What shall we wear?' For the Gentiles seek after all these things, and your heavenly Father knows that you need them all. But seek first the kingdom of God and his righteousness, and all these things will be added to you.*
>
> — Matthew 6:31-33

If we seek to please God, He will bless us in the ways He sees fit.

What We Do and Have

We can easily measure our success by one standard: what we've done with what we've been given.

You're probably familiar with the Parable of the Talents...

God

For it will be like a man going on a journey, who called his servants and entrusted to them his property. To one he gave five talents, to another two, to another one, to each according to his ability. Then he went away. He who had received the five talents went at once and traded with them, and he made five talents more. So also he who had the two talents made two talents more. But he who had received the one talent went and dug in the ground and hid his master's money. Now after a long time the master of those servants came and settled accounts with them. And he who had received the five talents came forward, bringing five talents more, saying, 'Master, you delivered to me five talents; here, I have made five talents more.' His master said to him, 'Well done, good and faithful servant. You have been faithful over a little; I will set you over much. Enter into the joy of your master.' And he also who had the two talents came forward, saying, 'Master, you delivered to me two talents; here, I have made two talents more.' His master said to him, 'Well done, good and faithful servant. You have been faithful over a little; I will set you over much. Enter into the joy of your master.' He also who had received the one talent came forward, saying, 'Master, I knew you to be a hard man, reaping where you did not sow, and gathering where you scattered no seed, so I was afraid, and I went and hid your talent in the ground. Here, you have what is yours.' But his master answered him, 'You wicked and slothful servant! You knew that I reap where I have not sown and gather where I scattered no seed? Then you ought to have invested my money with the bankers, and at my coming I should have received what was my own with interest. So take the talent from him and give it to him who has the ten talents. For to everyone who has will more be given, and he will have an abundance. But from the one who has not, even what he has will be taken away.

— Matthew 25:14-29

Straight from the mouth of Jesus. It's apparent, God measures our success by what we've done with what we've been given. So how does that apply today? If we have enough money to feed and clothe our family, we should be giving. It's arguable that we should be giving even if we don't. If we have a lot of free time, we should be spending a lot of time doing the work of Jesus.

Christians Are Different

As Christians, many parts of our life are backward from the rest of the world. Happiness is often idolized as the ultimate goal, yet as Christians, we should strive for joy over happiness. Joy in the fact that we are forgiven due to the work of Jesus.

Think about marriage. You may have heard before that marriage isn't supposed to make you happy, it's supposed to make you holy. Divorce is so common because people think marriage is meant purely to make us happy. As soon as someone is unhappy in their marriage, they think something must be wrong. But the truth is, that's normal, and we aren't always supposed to be happy every minute of every day.

However, we can be joyful. Even in prison, as Paul shows us, we can be joyful...

> *I thank my God in all my remembrance of you, always in every prayer of mine for you all making my prayer with joy, because of your partnership in the gospel from the first day until now. And I am sure of this, that he who began a good work in you will bring it to completion at the day of Jesus Christ. It is right for me to feel this way about you all, because I hold you in my heart, for you are all partakers with me of grace, both in my imprisonment and in the defense and confirmation of the gospel. For God is my witness, how I yearn for you all with the affection of Christ Jesus. And it is my prayer that your love may abound more and more, with knowledge and all discernment, so that you may approve what is excellent, and so be pure and blameless for the day of Christ, filled with the fruit of righteousness that comes through Jesus Christ, to the glory and praise of God.*
>
> — PHILIPPIANS 1:3-11

We are always to be growing in our faith and relationship with Christ, and that's where true joy sparks from. Along those same lines, we measure success differently from the rest of the world. And that's ok... it's actually a beautiful thing, because success measured by material wealth never leads to happiness or joy. It's ok to be different. As Christians, we should get used to it.

While there's nothing wrong with obtaining financial and business success, it shouldn't be the first category that comes into our head when we picture success.

I want to close this book with a practical section on studying your Bible and getting closer to God in the process. Let's talk about the Bible...

A Guide to Your Bible

There have been over six billion Bibles printed to date. There are well over 1,000 translations into new languages currently in progress. It's the most popular book in history, hands down. Ironically, it's also the most stolen book in history, but that's a different conversation. Granted, it's not really fair to other books, since it was written by God and it's technically 66 books, written by at least 40 different authors, over a 1,600-year period.

If that doesn't make the Bible appealing, there are plenty of other reasons to read it. I dare you to find any other 66 books written over a 1,000+ year period that have anything to do with each other, and here we have the Bible, which maintains the same theme over the course of almost a million words.

The Bible has been endorsed by Christians, Jews, and people who claim to be neither of the two. It's an amazing work to say the absolute least. I'll simply let N.T. Wright sum it up:

> "The Bible is the book of my life. It's the book I live with, the book I live by, the book I want to die by."

You probably already believe in the supernatural nature of the Bible, so let's get into how we can read the Bible for all of its worth and glory.

The Bible can be overwhelming. It's long, and quite frankly, some parts are boring. When we get into the begats, lineages, and census numbers, it's easy to lose focus. So how do we create a reading plan we actually stick with? What's a daily reading plan look like? You have to create your own method, and remember, a good reading plan you stick with is better than the best reading plan you don't. So let's get started…

1. Create Reading Time

We all have the same 24 hours in a day. How we use them is what's important. We can choose to use them watching TV or scrolling Facebook, or we can use the bulk of our hours to grow, learn, and get closer to God.

The first step in any Bible reading plan is to create a time block for it, but not just one. I actually have two backup time slots. I schedule my Bible reading every day at 4:00am. If I miss it for some reason, I try to catch up on a break at work. If I'm too busy to read it then, I'll read it during my regular reading time before bed.

I'm motivated to read it during the first time slot because I don't always have time for a break at work, and I like to have my reading time before bed to read other books. So create a time (preferably the *same time* every day) to read your Bible, and create a backup time slot for when you miss the first one. It's best for your backup slot to be slightly inconvenient, so you're motivated to finish it earlier.

2. Choose Your Translation

This is a debated topic, and it can get heated quickly. I've found that most of the popular translations are similar in many ways, and the best part is, you can always compare translations when you read (and you should).

When you're looking for the best translation, you should consider the different types:

- **Literal Translation** – This type of translation attempts to translate word-for-word, while keeping as close to the original meaning. This is also known as a transliteration. Examples include: *English Standard Version (ESV), King James and New King James Version (KJV and NKJV), New American Standard Bible (NASB), and Revised Standard Version (RSV)*.
- **Equivalent Translation** – This is more of a thought-for-thought translation. This type of translation attempts to read beyond one word at a time and give an overall idea of the entire context. Examples include: *New American Bible (NAB), New International Version (NIV), and Today's New International Version (TNIV)*.
- **Paraphrase Translation** – This type of

translation is less precise, but still usable and helpful in reading. It seeks to give you the meaning of the words, but of course, it's open to the translators' interpretation. Examples include: *Good News Translation (GNT), The Living Bible (TLB), The Message (MSG), and New Living Translation (NLT).*

All types of translations can be useful. There is no one-size-fits-all translation for every need. I'm going to go ahead and ease your nerves a little bit. You're not going to Hell for picking the "wrong" translation. There are advocates for every translation, and there are plenty of guides online to explain the differences.

Try a few versions until you find one you like that's been shown to be an accurate translation. It's important to get a solid translation, but just getting started is more important. I would recommend sticking with one primary translation so you can focus on your reading, but when you get stuck on a verse or want to study in greater depth, try reading a few different versions.

3. Find or Create a Plan

You can find a plan or create your own. There are plenty of awesome free plans out there if you're trying to read through the entire Bible in a year. There are plans to read through the entire Bible faster and slower than that as well, but a year is the most common plan.

These are the typical types of plans you'll find:

- **Beginning to End** (From Genesis to

Revelation)
- **Chronological** (In the order the events actually happened)
- **Historical** (In the order the books were written)
- **New, Then Old** (New Testament first, then the Old Testament)
- **Old and New** (Passages from the Old Testament and New Testament, each day)

If you want to create your own plan, simply choose a method, and stick with it. I wouldn't suggest spending the time to actually create your own plan that's exactly a year long, I would recommend creating a reading plan with four different sections.

Here's the most common way to divide your daily reading:

1. Read one chapter from Psalms
2. Read one chapter from Proverbs
3. Read one chapter from the Old Testament
4. Read one chapter from the New Testament

That's a good foundation. Read one chapter a day from each section. If you can read more, great! If you can only read the one chapter, that's totally fine.

If you don't want to read that much each day or if you don't have the time right now, consider a daily devotional. Devotionals are a great way to read the Bible each day in just a few minutes. You can find plenty of devotionals at any book store, and for free online.

4. Define Your Reading Goal

I'm not talking about setting goals to read a certain amount of pages, though that's a good idea too. I'm talking about your desired outcome. Do you simply want to *read* the Bible? Or do you want to *study* the Bible? If you want to study it, do you want to study verse-by-verse, chapter-by-chapter, or do you want to get down to word-by-word?

5. Write in Your Bible

The Bible is holy, but that doesn't mean you can't underline, highlight, and write in it. You may have noticed some people's Bibles are full of notes and writing. While some people do it because they think it makes them look more holy (I've been guilty of this), it really is a great way to dive deeper into the Word.

There are some great methods out there to help guide you. You could use colored pencils and use different colors for underlining specific topics. You could draw symbols beside certain Scriptures that signify further study. Or you can simply underline verses that jump out at you. There's no right or wrong. Just start and see where it goes.

6. Open With Prayer

There's no better way to start your Bible reading than by saying a simple prayer. This is a great way to relax and focus on what you're doing. I always pray for three things when I start my daily reading:

1. **Peace** – Ask for the peace and quiet to devote your entire mind to the reading at hand. Ask God to help you focus on what you're reading, instead of letting your mind drift.
2. **Revelation Knowledge** – I pray God will make the Scriptures come alive in new ways and that He will help me gain new knowledge and understanding, even if I have read this verse 1,000 times.
3. **God's Will** – Ask God to show you how to apply your reading to your life. We're all going through a different time and season, and God's Word is applicable to whatever time we're in.

Don't get caught up on saying the right things. God listens when you pray, and thankfully, He knows your heart. He's not waiting on you to pray the "right" words.

7. Use Multiple Mediums

Use a physical Bible, an audio Bible, or whichever mediums work for you, and use them together. This is an extra step that can be extremely helpful. Though it's not technically part of your reading plan, it will help you commit verses to memory and absorb more of the Bible.

Look for an audio bible. I actually prefer listening to a different translation from what I read to get a broader perspective. You can have it playing in your car on your commute, on road trips, or any time you can listen.

You can find plenty of great audio Bibles online – many for free!

8. Ask Yourself Questions

There's a reason teachers give tests. It's to help the students better understand the subject and to help the information stick. Think of this as a personal test you give yourself after each reading, but don't worry, you can't fail this test! Here's how it works...

Create a list with at least one question and no more than three. This will be a short list of things you can ask yourself after each reading session. It's a great way to get the most out of your reading (it works with other books as well).

You could choose any of the following questions (or create your own):

- What was the key idea behind that chapter?
- What was the overall message of your reading?
- How can you apply what you just read in your life?
- What did all of the chapters you read have in common?
- What are the similarities and differences between you and the people you just read about?

Now create your own list! I say no more than three questions because you will be more likely to do it every time, and it won't take long. You can jot the answer(s) down in your journal or you could always start a separate journal just for your Bible reading.

9. Study Your Patterns

This is extremely important. Be realistic. Study your patterns and honestly discern whether or not your method is working. For example, if you decided two months ago that 5:00am is the best time for you to read your Bible, but you've only actually got up at 5:00am twice in two months, you may want to rethink your method. This goes back to what we talked about in chapter 9: self-awareness.

You may be a night owl. You may be a morning person. You may prefer to read on your lunch break. You may prefer to read before bed. Whatever keeps you consistent, do that. You may even find that you can't consistently read the Bible, but you keep the audio Bible in your car... and that's great! If you find nothing is working for you, the issue may be more with your discipline and level of commitment, which we discussed in chapter 2.

10. Keep Going

Once you have a method, start reading and keep reading. You may be surprised how much you enjoy reading your Bible when you have a system. I used to always struggle with my Bible reading, because I was never really sure of my intent. Was I reading to read or reading to study? I never really knew. Once I defined it, it was much easier.

What happens if you miss a day? The Bible will still be there tomorrow. The best time to pick back up is right now. Don't feel guilty for missing it, just start where you left off. If I miss a few days, it will take a few more days to catch up, but once I'm caught back up, everything goes back to normal.

The main point of this section is this: read your Bible. You don't need a perfect plan to get started. Plans are great and necessary, but if you're waiting on the perfect plan, stop waiting and start reading.

Summary & Action

Life works when God is at the center.

- *Who is at the center of your life?*

You should have a reading plan that works for you.

- *Are you searching for a plan?*

Use the type of Bible that fits your needs.

- *Are you using a physical Bible, audio, or both?*

Action: Create a daily Bible reading plan. Find the time for daily prayer. Let God into your life, and watch your life become fruitful in ways you never imagined.
Reflection:

AFTERWORD

No book is ever going to teach you everything you need to know. Most of what you need to know likely won't come from a book at all. We learn more from life, mentors, trials, successes, mistakes, and unexpected events than we could ever learn from a book. That being said, books are extremely valuable to our growth. They allow us to learn from other people's lives, successes, and failures. That's extremely valuable.

My hope is that you've learned something here (hopefully a whole lot of something!). When combined, the 10 branches of life make up our existence and let us live the fruitful life we're all looking for. We can control these 10 areas as much as we can respond appropriately.

We all have the same 10 branches of life.

We're all in this together.

Let's grow together.

RECOMMENDED READING

Books Referenced, in Order:

- *Grit: The Power of Passion and Perseverance* by Angela Duckworth
- *Beyond Grit: Ten Powerful Practices to Gain the High-Performance Edge* by Cindra Kamphoff
- *Tiny Habits: The Small Changes That Change Everything* by BJ Fogg
- *Getting Things Done: The Art of Stress-Free Productivity* by David Allen
- *How to Stop Worrying and Start Living* by Dale Carnegie

Additional Recommended Books:

- *A Random Walk Down Wall Street: The Time-Tested Strategy for Successful Investing* by Burton G. Malkiel
- *Atomic Habits: An Easy and Proven Way to Build Good Habits and Break Bad Ones* by James Clear
- *Better Than Good: Creating a Life You Can't Wait to Live* by Zig Ziglar
- *Crucial Conversations: Tools for Talking When Stakes are High* by Grenny, McMillan, Patterson & Switzler
- *Eat That Frog! 21 Great Ways to Stop*

Procrastinating and Get More Done in Less Time by Brian Tracy
- *How to Have Confidence and Power in Dealing With People* by Les Giblin
- *How to Win Friends and Influence People* by Dale Carnegie
- *Leading an Inspired Life* by Jim Rohn
- *Mindset: The New Psychology of Success* by Carol S. Dweck
- *Procrastinate on Purpose: 5 Permissions to Multiply Your Time* by Rory Vaden
- *The 4-Hour Workweek: Escape 9-5, Live Anywhere, and Join the New Rich* by Timothy Ferriss
- *The Five Love Languages: The Secret to Love That Lasts* by Gary Chapman
- *The Magic of Thinking Big* by David J. Schwartz
- *The More of Less* by Joshua Becker
- *The Power of Habit: Why We Do What We Do in Life and Business* by Charles Duhigg
- *The Slight Edge: Turning Simple Disciplines Into Massive Success and Happiness* by Jeff Olson
- *The Total Money Makeover: A Proven Plan for Financial Fitness* by Dave Ramsey

ABOUT THE AUTHOR

Kalen is a financial coach, author, and active-duty servicemember. He holds a BA in Finance, but admits he's learned more from books than any degree.

Kalen is the founder of Freedom Sprout, a project to cultivate financial freedom for future generations. He has a mission to raise a generation of children who are financially literate, and help others do the same. Kalen has been writing in the finance and productivity world since 2013. His work has been featured on *Yahoo! Finance*, *CNN Money*, *The Globe and Mail*, *The Penny Hoarder*, and *WiseBread*, among major other online publications and magazines. He has been married to his wife, Tiffany, since 2005. They have five children, and currently live in and travel through Europe regularly.

For more of Kalen's writing, visit FreedomSprout.com.

facebook.com/freedomsprout
twitter.com/sproutfreedom

NOTES

2. Discipline

1. Is Willpower a Limited Resource? American Psychological Association.

5. Energy

1. Warner, J. (2006). Exercise Fights Fatigue, Boosts Energy. WebMD.
2. Parker-Pope, T. (2008). The Cure for Exhaustion? More Exercise. The New York Times.

6. Time

1. Average Time Spent Daily on Social Media. BroadbandSearch.
2. C, Mims. (2011) Stop Organizing Your E-Mail, Study Says. MIT Technology Review.

7. Wealth

1. Remember, an emergency fund should be figured by using a bare-bones lifestyle. If you lost your job today, you wouldn't keep spending $1,000/month on eating out.
2. A, Riquier. (2019). More Evidence That Passive Fund Management Beats Active. MarketWatch.

9. Self

1. Frone, M. (2000). Work-Family Conflict and Employee Psychiatric Disorders. *Journal of Applied Psychology*. 85(6), 888-895.

2. J, Hoffman. (2013). How Meditation Might Boost Your Test Scores. The New York Times.
3. Yale University. (2005). Meditation Associated With Increased Grey Matter in the Brain. ScienceDaily.
4. Cahn, B. R., & Polich, J. (2006). Meditation states and traits: EEG, ERP, and neuroimaging studies. *Psychological Bulletin*. 132(2), 180–211.

www.ingramcontent.com/pod-product-compliance
Lightning Source LLC
Chambersburg PA
CBHW030323080526
44584CB00012B/678

the end of everything and the masculine is just an attribute supporting this universal phenomenon.

Divine feminine:
It exists within all of us

The irony of today's world is that we only see one half of the truth which is the secondary and dependent half. We have in fact become blind to the primary and independent aspect of the truth. As a result of this anomaly and its consequence in the form of uncontrolled manifestation of the masculine principle, we can see great imbalance in the universe.

All the chaos and destruction that we are seeing today is the result of this anomaly and imbalance.

To restore the balance of the universe we need to rekindle the divine feminine that actually exists in all of us. That which exists within us has to be called upon and expressed within our own inner self as well as the external universe.

Only this energy can propel us towards the true direction and purpose of our life. The Mantra is to achieve a balance in life by evoking the feminine and move towards the path of ultimate liberation. Once we start achieving the balance within our own inner self, then it starts manifesting in our relationships with others and the world at large. This is the only way to bring back the balance in the universe.

CHAPTER 4

WHOLE BRAIN THINKING

For thousands of years we have looked out to the heavens or inside ourselves to contemplate God's nature. In the process of seeking into a vast emptiness we have forgotten about the sacred power of the present moment which is creatively happening through us and in the world around us. It is time for us all to move beyond culture's left brain focus on a disembodied and transcendent God, a focus which has split apart spirit and matter. It is time to bring back the fullness of all that exists.

In Western cultures women and men are taught to live in their minds (left brain) and to doubt their own intuitive and instinctive knowledge (right brain). By primarily valuing the left brain hemisphere, we become disconnected from our bodies and from nature and we limit our potential creativity and our intellectual flexibility to fully experience and understand our lives and the world.

Whole Brain Thinking - Honoring the Divine Feminine

How can we understand and experience the nature of God in the Divine Feminine aspects of fullness and love while still honoring Divine Masculine aspects of emptiness and freedom? We can begin by becoming more consciously aware in daily life. Then, as we mature and evolve in skill and wisdom, we will learn to connect with the eternal, cosmic mind of God. Most will find that they have reversed this process because of our culture's predominate focus on a distant God who dwells in Heaven. Either path still leads to the One so that the essential task is to combine and then integrate the two aspects of God to form one whole, non-dual perspective.

What is Whole Braining Thinking?

Whole brain thinking is the ability to use both the left and the right brain adeptly. The corpus callosum facilitates this connection - a large band of neural fibers that connects the two cerebral hemispheres. This connecting band of tissue in women is thicker than in men, raising the question, *"How is a woman's way of experiencing God going to be influenced by this thicker bridge between the two hemispheres?"*

Because women have an enhanced ability to use both left and right brain hemispheres, women have the most to offer in healing the split between the masculine way of understanding

God (emptiness and freedom) with the feminine way of understanding God (fullness, love and the present moment).

What is the Divine Feminine Way to God?

The feminine is the core of creation that is love. Creation, love and the Divine Feminine are one and the same. Every woman instinctively knows that she is at the center of this great creative mystery that is unfolding in the moment. The Divine Feminine aspects of God put us in touch with our own bodies, our own imagery and our own truth and in so doing we awaken to what is meaningful in our lives. She values all things as important to the health of the whole and recognizes our mutual connectedness. Her fearless embrace of feeling in the present moment can remind us of the incredible mystery and sacred power of life.

"Non-dual realization embraces both emptiness (masculine) and matter/form (feminine) aspects. "Being" and "becoming" are both parts of a non-dual, self realization.»

What Does the Divine Feminine Value?

The Divine Feminine values all matter - living beings and nonliving natural objects and also every part of all things - as important to the health of the whole. She recognizes our mutual interdependence and connectedness to all things for survival, well-being and evolutionary vibrancy. She places a great deal of significance on having good relationships based on mutual cooperation and she uses intuitive, instinctive knowledge.

Moving Into Whole Brain Thinking

When women and men remember what the Divine Feminine really values, we realize we must include all perspectives to gain an understanding of the wholeness and connectedness of life. To do so we must dive fearlessly into the mystery of the pain and suffering that is part of the great feminine initiation into the cycles of creation.

We honor the Great Mother Goddess when we embrace life as it is. She embodies the wisdom of forgiveness and turns us to what is hidden in darkness to be reborn in a powerful new way. We can then focus on the present moment where anything is possible and no separation exists if we listen to and respond courageously to our intuitive wisdom.

With greater understanding of the differences between right and left brain thinking and appreciation of what the divine feminine values, we have the opportunity to return to the beneficial wholeness of both the masculine (ascending) and feminine (descending) aspects of God united in oneness.

Integrating Divine Feminine and Masculine Principles Into Your Life Reawakening to the divine feminine is a union of embodying her principles in our daily lives as well as intellectually integrating and including the bright light of masculine consciousness. We combine these two by:

> **1.** Enjoying the world with our five senses while using our sixth sense - intuitive knowledge. Intuitive knowledge makes something known by focusing our attention on universal knowledge or collective consciousness.

> **2.** Seeing the parts then integrating and combining them to form a whole. Western cultures teach the scientific method of separating the parts from the whole and calling them truth. As we broaden

our knowledge, we learn that just because something looks true, doesn't mean it's the only truth or absolute truth.

3. Being and Becoming - learning to meditate, pray or contemplate while staying in present time, in our bodies, for our own needs as well as the moment's.

4. Traveling deeply into space to experience emptiness, oneness and freedom and then returning and going deeply into the cycles and mystery of creation in order to become empowered and reborn in a new way. We can master ascending (masculine way to God) and descending (feminine way to God) at the same time.

Exercises for Becoming More Whole Brained People use to say if you were logical, you were definitely left-brained, and if you were creative, you were definitely right-brained.

This is no longer the case. New research indicates that there's more flexibility in our brains and we can train our brains to become more organized, creative or better able to process all sorts of information. Knowing where our strengths and weaknesses are can help us strengthen the weaker hemisphere. Here are some ways to strengthen the left or right hemispheres:

Left Brain Exercises

1. Make lists

One method of getting into details is to outline what must be done. Bite sized chunks of daily tasks are an excellent way to engage the left hemisphere and also to overcome apparently impossible hurdles.

2. Pay attentions to details

The left hemisphere is about details and linear thinking. Notice the details in the surrounding environment and connect to what is happening through the power of observation.

3. Change your immediate environment

Changing surroundings is an opportunity to change thinking because the mind will not have its familiar environment to cue it into old habits. Create an environment that has beautiful, calming, and enjoyable details.

Right Brain Exercises

1. Keep the bigger picture in mind

Take time to become aware of the greater scheme of life and larger reoccurring patterns.

2. Creative visualization

Learn to quit the chatter in the mind and to allow the spatial, holistic and much more unconscious right brain do its work. Meditation and contemplative practices are useful techniques to quit the left brain.

3. Practice spatial rotation exercises

The right brain is involved in spatial tasks as well as holistic vision. Imagine objects rotating in space. Keep a clear image of the object while it is moving.

4. Learn to trust intuitive information

Allow the right brain the opportunity to function by reflecting on unique and creative thoughts. Honor the insights received through day dreams, visions and imaginings. Relax and enjoy their creative possibilities.

CHAPTER 5

THE RETURN OF THE FEMININE

Visionaries, luminaries, modern mystics along with more practical thought leaders found in every field including, economists, business people and environmentalists, as well as everyday people, have made a claim that 2017 is the year of this paradigm shift. This new energy is the return of the Divine Soul's Feminine Energy.

We are in just the beginning of a long new cycle of a new vibration alignment in which everything including our very essence, our souls is in a huge awakening time. While this is exciting news, it is also transitional and that is often unsettling as the balance that once was is no longer and a new normal is being formed. It will take a very long time to see the overall results but everyday when we act in courage we are co-creating this new normal. The over all shift is from the patriarch to equality between it and the matriarch. The new vibration, involves the divine soul's fememine energy flow. What is the Divine Soul's Feminine energy?

The energy of the Divine Feminine is a unique and natural experience.. Unique in that the feminine energy is present in anything or anyone, including men when they are nourishing and sustaining life. The feminine energy is automatically plugged into being connected to others. Women as holders of that energy hold a genuine authentic capacity of empathy for one another's a challenges, and to encourage and nurture each others hidden potential. Life is sustainable when this happens.

It is what the feminine energy does so well. It sustains and fills our empty buckets with the kind of juice and zest we need to carry on and carry out our desires. Everything that is life affirming and sustaining is the Divine Feminine Energy. Carrying and facilitating this energy is the highest value of women's work during her lifetime. With its help we can activate a new age of human possibilities and potential for ways of being that we haven't even dreamt yet.

We are in the midst of the shift from the ego to the essence of ourselves; our soul's awakening and participating in our daily lives in bigger ways. It is the soul over matter and heart over the head mindset-shift that demands new tools and training so we can become aligned to these shifts and changes. It's either, evolve or we as a species may die.

Humanity is being taken to the point where it will have to choose between suicide and adoration. It will be a breaking point in having to set a new course in our economic, political and environmental but most importantly we as individuals have to step into our greatest fears our own brilliance and do those things that we are feeling the urge to do.

This is a unique time in history in which the balance of our very planet is awakening to make the shift to the Divine Soul's feminine flow to sustain and learn to live from our heart and soul. Make the decision to cross over the threshold into personal transformation and personal healing so that your gifts can claim a stake in a new space.

You are an important piece of the larger picture. New ways of relating to one another on this planet are being birthed as we surrender and align to the energy of the Divine Soul's Feminine flow. Each of us can become powerful change.

How can you begin to implement the divine energy of the feminine in your life?

Call in the divine feminine energy into your lives by asking the miracle, the magic, and the mystery to be a part of your daily life and for your business.

Remove isolation. Sure it is okay to allow yourself time to work through a sticky point but after 3 days, reach out and get help. Asking for help is the way the divine feminine can come through your friend or mentor and give you just the boost what you need to get back on track.

CHAPTER 6

FEMININE POWER

At a party, you see a woman or man across the room with a charisma that is out of this world. On the street, you notice a woman or man walking towards you with a stride that leaves you in awe. At work, you watch the new sales manager address everyone with such finesse and ease that you feel envy creeping up your spine. At a restaurant, your eye catches a voluptuous vixen flirting with the waiter with such ease and it leaves you wondering, how does he or she do that? What do all of these people have in common?

They possess the power of the feminine. This type of Mystical Radiance permeates and radiates from people who are anchored within their body. Their energy speaks volumes and they need not say a word.

These people have no need to be loud, to display or solicit attention from others. Their power is not dependent on outside forces; they have developed their inner forces to feed, nourish and serve them. They rely on inner resources for counsel, guidance and directives. They have lifted the veils of delusional feminine ideology and integrated the essence of authentic feminine energy. These people did not arrive to such a destination without peril. They struggled, wept, despaired and rose from the ashes like a phoenix.

Feminine power in the 21st century is still misunderstood, often times by women themselves. I have witnessed women behave in such inappropriate ways when it came to beauty, men, money and popularity. It is as if on a subliminal level of the feminine soul has been convinced that the bread crumbs tossed her way could satisfy her immense nature.

Lack of personal power is a learned behavior. Some of us learn from our parents, grandparents or other relatives who populate our family tree. We absorb subliminal messages from them to settle for less in the realm of money, career, and relationships.

In subliminal ways, we are encouraged to stay just like them. However, each generation is destined to break free from such limitations and begin the journey to self-realization. It is a monumental task but one worth undertaking.

Certain religions and societies around the world expect nothing more from a woman than her ability to bear children. In this societal or religious group, a woman can only fulfill her biological destiny and nothing more. She will not be allowed to develop her Divine Feminine potential.

Instead, she will be encouraged to give her power away and compromise her identity in the process.

In society, women are taught from a young age to grow up and be the perfect woman. They are expected to do it all and if they can't do it all, there is something wrong. Theye are taught that everything in the world is limited - finances, jobs, men, love, promotions, etc. They are told that sex is the only weapon they have to ensure they get what they want.

They are told self-sacrifice is a noble act. They are told that a woman's worth depends on who she marries, where she lives, the size of the rock on her finger, the children she bears, the car she drives, where she shops, the champagne she drinks, and of course, her dress size.

Society has devised so many distractions for the modern woman to keep her from owning her power. Women are expected to hide their intelligence, their power and their strength in order to remain in good favor with the men in their lives. Being influenced by these voices and believing them limits a woman's sense of individuality. So many try to live by these standards only to discover the monster of discontentment is lurking just beneath the surface. The modern woman lives in a time where her possibilities are endless and her potential ripe. All this freedom has not contributed to her happiness but has been the cause of her confusion.

The feminine face of God has enough influence to veto the patriarchal brand of power. However, rarely has this been the case. Women through the centuries were taught to solicit affections from man but to care nothing about his integrity or moral character. They allowed his unsavory conduct and failed to hold him accountable. The ancient sisters were not in a position to draw the line but now they are.

For every woman who holds the people in her life accountable teaches them to be mindful in the future of thought, word and deed. Every time a woman says 'This is unacceptable' to her lovers, friends and family, she helps to straighten out the fabric of her being and that of the collective.

Also, Women need to reclaim being treated like ladies and learn to walk away when it's otherwise. Women need to develop, what I call, emotional backbone. When you have emotional backbone, you no longer operate on fear but fearlessness. if you speak your truth you know your chronic headaches will disappear.

Women must learn to rely on the higher self for all the things they currently want from others.

This draws people to you not because the energy you exude piques curiosity or makes people feel amazing in your presence. They can't get enough of you and remember you haven't even done anything. You are simply being your higher self. Just being you is enough to receive, warm smiles and flattering compliments without the need to be outrageous or to hide your magnificence. A word to the wise, seek out self-realized women and men try to learn from them. They have been in your shoes, they have struggled with the questions and their lives mirror the answers. They know the terrain by heart and can guide your footsteps.

CHAPTER 7

SURRENDERING TO DIVINE FEMININE

One of the greatest opportunities and challenges for men or women in this day and age is surrendering to the Divine Feminine. The current state of humanity as a civilization and the world we live in is a reflection of the collective consciousness that has been dominant for thousands of years.

One particular aspect of this collective consciousness has been the distorted and domineering aspect of the masculine energy within society. The polar opposite effect of the dominant masculine energy has been the repression of the feminine energy both within ourselves and through the outer manifestations of reality.

Nothing has been more devastating towards the evolution and ascension of humanity to a higher state of consciousness based on love, cooperation and oneness than the Masculine-Feminine Rift. And the only way to transcend and heal this evolutionary impediment is for humanity to experience the surrendering to the Divine Feminine. This surrender can only occur within ourselves and requires more than a shift of belief systems and ways of thinking, it requires a re-patterning of our DNA.

Let's first start by describing some of the energy signatures or qualities of masculine and feminine energies:

Masculine Energy	Feminine Energy
Action	Presence
Control and Righteousness	Surrender
Manifested Matter	Unmanifested Matter (Void/Source)
Competition	Cooperation/Support
Provider	Nurture
Rational	Intuition/Emotional Intelligence

Whether you are a man or a woman, you have ALL of these energies within you, yet your gender will greatly determine which energies will tend to be expressed more through your physiology (brain, hormones, body figure, voice tonality), emotions, mental constructions and soul vibration.

Despite having all these energies within, most of humanity has revolved for some time now around in what appears to be a masculine energy dominant world where outer success and worldly achievements are valued more than intuition, where emotional expression equals weakness, where the greatness of motherhood has been diminished and where competition, greed for power and the need for control have taken over the joy and grace of life/existence itself.

The first step to balance these inner masculine and feminine energies is to release the Pride and or Ego. There is nothing wrong with a feeling of pride for having done a good job, etc. but when you live for your pride, that's when it can become a problem. When you are constantly fueling the ego, it is like chasing an illusive dragon or trying to quench an unending thirst.

The ego must constantly be filled with pride to make the host feel okay. However, there is nothing wrong with the host feeling okay. The difference is in the motivation. Living for pride alone is an addiction of sorts that stems from a place that feels less than or un-whole, in my personal layperson's perspective.

If one is seeking the ego feed of pride alone to feel good, know that the action will only ever result in a short-lived high of sorts. However, other pursuits from a more healthy place will have longer lasting results - like being kind to self and others just for the opportunity itself to be kind. That feels good but to take too much pride in that and to hold yourself above others in that is where the motivation comes into focus.

So, I would say that you don't need to ditch your pride but just don't let it stand between you and what is most beautiful and magical in life. This is exactly what I am doing with this e-book it will assist people to embody their Higher Self and heal the Male-Female Rift (this healing session is available to everyone). This is the most important and crucial step to take for any person who desire to balance their inner masculine and feminine energies and experience a re-birth in consciousness. Once this step is taken the next step consists in expressing that inner balance through your outer reality.

In my own relationship my dominant masculine energies and the repressed feminine energies manifested mainly through the need to be right, the need to control and repressing my emotions. Therefore my Higher Self guided me to make a conscious decision and develop new ways of being where I:

- Drop my sense of self-righteousness and the need to control everything
- Honor her voice and opinions
- Honor her emotions and hold a safe space for her to express them
- Honor my own emotions and express them in functional and healthy ways

These conscious actions have resulted in greater intuition, enhanced emotional intelligence, greater sense of compassion, becoming more empathic, enhanced energy healing abilities, greater state of presence and deepening the states of allowing.

When it comes to women, some have repressed their Divine Feminine energies in order to exalt their masculine energies in hopes to survive in this male dominated world. The women who consciously, subconsciously or unconsciously choose to repress their feminine energies will often adopt the masculine traits of competition, control and the need for external power.

What do you think happens when a woman who has repressed her feminine energies and now has overactive masculine energies gets into a relationship with a man who has a dominant masculine energy? Fights, arguments and power struggles will manifest constantly in the relationship.

So when the man is able to surrender to the Divine Feminine and the woman surrenders to the Divine Masculine, the woman can drop the need to control everything, including sex, and the male finally can relax and drop the whole facade to try to impress her with success, money and power.

The ultimate result is a relationship where both partners can hold and own their corresponding balanced ratio of masculine and feminine energies, creating a magnetic attraction and celebration of their own uniqueness and differences.

www.ingramcontent.com/pod-product-compliance
Lightning Source LLC
Chambersburg PA
CBHW052118070526
44584CB00017B/2544